REA

ACPL

DISCARDED

ALLEN COUNTY PUBLIC

3 1833 0037

D0917155

A HATFUL OF RAIN

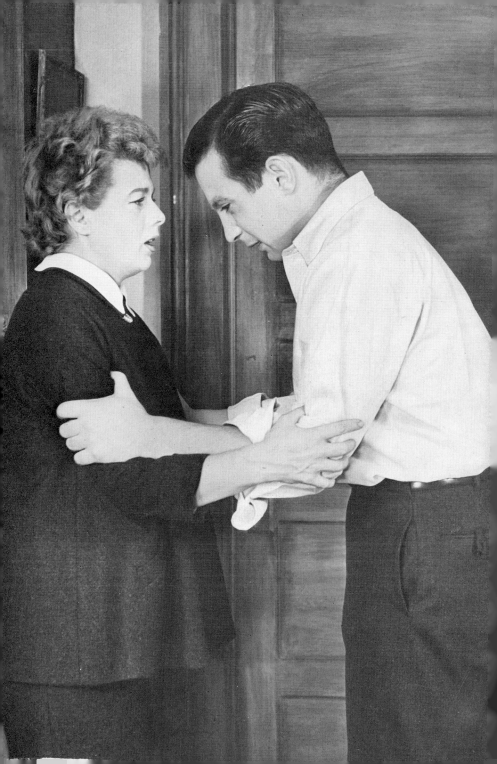

A Hatful
of Rain

by Michael Vincente Gazzo

Random House
New York

COPYRIGHT, AS AN UNPUBLISHED WORK, 1954,
BY MICHAEL V. GAZZO

© COPYRIGHT, 1956, BY MICHAEL V. GAZZO

All rights including the right of reproduction in whole or in part, in any form, are reserved under International and Pan-American Copyright Conventions. Published in New York by Random House, Inc. and simultaneously in Toronto, Canada, by Random House of Canada, Limited.

CAUTION: *Professionals and amateurs are hereby warned that* A HATFUL OF RAIN *being fully protected under the Copyright Laws of the United States of America, the British Empire, including the Dominion of Canada, and all other countries of the Copyright Union, is subject to royalty. All rights, including professional, amateur, motion picture, recitation, lecturing, public reading, radio and television broadcasting, and the rights of translation into foreign languages are strictly reserved. Particular emphasis is laid on the question of readings, permission for which must be secured from the author's agent in writing. All inquiries should be addressed to the author's agent, Audrey Wood, M.C.A. Artists Ltd., 598 Madison Avenue, New York, N.Y.*

FIRST PRINTING

Photographs by courtesy of Leo Friedman

Library of Congress Catalog Card Number: 56–8050

MANUFACTURED IN THE
UNITED STATES OF AMERICA

To My Fathers

Michael and David

1999127

A HATFUL OF RAIN was first presented by Jay Julien at the Lyceum Theatre, New York City, on November 9, 1955, with the following cast:

(IN ORDER OF APPEARANCE)

JOHN POPE, SR.	Frank Silvera
JOHNNY POPE	Ben Gazzara
CELIA POPE	Shelley Winters
MOTHER	Henry Silva
APPLES	Paul Richards
CHUCH	Harry Guardino
POLO POPE	Anthony Franciosa
MAN	Steve Gravers
PUTSKI	Christine White

Directed by Frank Corsaro

Production designed by Mordecai Gorelik

SCENES

The action takes place in a remodeled apartment on New York's Lower East Side.

ACT ONE

Scene   I: Early evening.
Scene II: Very late that night.

ACT TWO

Scene   I: Early the next morning.
Scene II: A few hours later.
Scene III: Early the same evening.

ACT THREE

Several hours later.

ACT ONE

ACT ONE

SCENE I

A tenement apartment on New York's Lower East Side. To our left we see a small kitchen, and to our right a combination living room-bedroom. There are two doors in the kitchen—one leading to the hallway, left, and the other, in the rear wall, leading to a bedroom. Looking through the living-room windows, we see the worn brick of the building next door and—beyond the fire-escape railing, which is just outside—distant window lights that outline a suspension bridge, marred only by the occasional suggestion of rooftops with jutting black chimneys.

It is only because of what is seen from these windows that we can place the apartment in the Lower East Side. Within the apartment itself there is everywhere the suggestion of a ceaseless effort to transform bedraggled rooms into rooms of comfort and taste. All the woodwork—formerly coated with twenty coats of paint—has been scraped, cleaned, stained and varnished. The windows have been refurbished; cases have been built beneath them, and they are spotlessly clean, as are the shades and draw curtains. Though the sink-and-tub combination is outdated in design, plywood has been used to cover up the intricacies of old-fashioned piping. Between the kitchen and bedroom, a partition of shelving has been built, and on each shelf are flowerpots, some of glass, others of copper, containing green plants. There is a sense of life.

In the kitchen, we see a cupboard, its paint removed, a table and four chairs. The chairs are old—picked up from one of the antique shops along Third Avenue. The table is solid and of heavy wood, something that might have been picked up from a farmer along a Jersey road.

In the living room, we see an armchair in a corner and a bed against the side wall. There is an unusual and startling use of color in the room; the bedspread is particularly lively, and all the objects in the room are colorful. Homemade bookcases made of wood planks and bricks line another wall.

The hallway, off the kitchen, is clearly in contrast to the apartment. Its walls are a drab brown and, off it, we see a suggestion of a stairway, leading to the roof, the railing of painted iron. Overhead there is a dim light, covered with a dusty and cracked skylight.

When the curtain rises, we hear the sound of rain. In the kitchen area, at the table, are JOHNNY *and his* FATHER. *The meal is almost at an end.*

FATHER

(*Moves away from the table, toward an umbrella which he picks up and works with difficulty, opening it and closing it*)

I almost missed the plane up because of this umbrella . . . it's made of Japanese silk, the handle is ivory . . . and it was designed in Germany . . . and they make the damn things in Peru. This guy down in Palm Beach who sold me the thing . . . Anyway, I kept looking at my watch. He wouldn't tell me how

4

much it was . . . I thought he was crazy until he told me the price. Twenty-seven dollars for an umbrella . . . Seven minutes from plane time he tells me the price . . .

JOHNNY

(*Calls off to* CELIA, *who is in* POLO's *room*)
Honey! What's the trouble in there?

CELIA

(*Stands in the doorway*)
I can't get Polo's windows closed. . . .

FATHER

Polo? That's Polo's room?

CELIA

Johnny . . . ? I can't close his windows and his bed is going to float out here any minute. The dampness has them jammed.
. . .

FATHER

I thought you and Johnny slept in there—and Polo slept out here.

CELIA

That room isn't big enough for two people. Johnny and I tried to sleep in there but—

FATHER

What are you going to call him?

CELIA

Her. Not him. Her.

FATHER

I was counting on a grandson.

CELIA

Well, you'll have to settle for a granddaughter.

FATHER

Wow! Whew . . . That's strong coffee. Turkish?

CELIA

No, it's not Turkish. It's just plain ordinary everyday coffee.

JOHNNY

What did you put in that pot?

CELIA

I don't understand it. Last night I put nine tablespoons of coffee in the pot and it came out like weak tea.

6

JOHNNY

Which pot? You know you got four pots and they're all different sizes . . .

CELIA

Well, I didn't ask for all those pots.

JOHNNY

If you'd just put three of those pots away—

CELIA

It's a curse, that's all. For as long as I could remember I could never make coffee . . .

JOHNNY

They gave her four pots . . . one of those showers when we got married.

CELIA

And you went out and bought one too—so never mind.

JOHNNY

How did I know that all your girl friends were coffee-pot happy. There were only six girls at the shower, and four of them show up with a coffee pot.

7

CELIA

This morning I had a headache—and I wanted to have my coffee, and I dropped an Alka Seltzer in my coffee. I thought for a minute the house was going to blow up . . .

FATHER

Sorry, honey, I didn't mean to knock your coffee.

CELIA

It's not you, Pop. I was late for work this morning . . . I had to go to the doctor's on my lunch hour—and I took a bus on the way back . . . and the bus had to wait ten minutes at an intersection while a parade passed by . . .

JOHNNY

Honey, you're behaving like a woman.

CELIA

Darling, if you'll just take a good look at me, you'll confirm the fact that I am a woman.

FATHER

What's this your wife writes me, you're not going to school any more . . .

JOHNNY

I'm going to start again soon, Pop. Working days and school nights, I—

FATHER

I don't want you to think that I'm pushing you, but I was down there feeling good about the fact that you got the government picking up the bill with that G.I. Rights thing . . . How long will it take you to finish, I mean if you started soon again . . . ?

CELIA

Another two years and he'll have his degree . . . Excuse me, Pop, I've got some ironing to do for work.

FATHER

Working in a machine shop, being a toolmaker, that must help you with engineering studies, huh?

JOHNNY

I'm a machinist, Pop. I'm not a toolmaker . . .

FATHER

You lost two years in the Army, another damn year laying in a hospital bed, now that's a big chunk of time—so look to the clock, Johnny.

JOHNNY

I was going to write and tell you myself about my not going to school any more, but I didn't want to worry you—

FATHER

You don't have any pains, I mean, you're all cured.

JOHNNY

Yeh, I'm all cured . . .

FATHER

Sometimes things like that act up . . . you know, guys with rheumatism, their teeth start to hurt when it rains. I'm just asking you . . .

JOHNNY

I'm all right, Pop.

FATHER

I was proud of you, Johnny. I told everybody down the Club . . . how you laid in a cave for thirteen days. I showed them that picture you took at the hospital . . . I told them all— how you went down to ninety pounds. How you kept your mouth shut, no matter what they did to you.

JOHNNY

Aw, come on now, Pop—there's nothing to be proud of.

CELIA

You'd think it was something to be ashamed of.

JOHNNY

Can we just forget about it . . . ?

FATHER

Well, I couldn't have held out—and I don't think there are many men who could. And I'm proud of you, kid!

JOHNNY

All right, Pop, you're proud of me.

CELIA

He tore up all the newspaper clippings. . . .

JOHNNY

Honey, will you please forget it?

FATHER

It's really coming down . . . every time I think of having to get on that plane tomorrow my stomach starts doing flip flops. . . . We got a glass wall they just put in, the sun comes in and from behind the bar you can see the water. Exclusive, private, only for the big wheels. Corporation lawyers, senators, department-store heads and a few judges thrown in. It was a good job. Well, maybe I can get it back.

JOHNNY

You mean you quit your job?

FATHER

What do you think I was shouting about before. Your brother wrote me a hundred times. Pop, I've got twenty-five hundred stashed away. Any time you want it, it's yours. I put money down on the option, and I started the renovations. The carpenters have been working there for a week, and I got the plumbers fixing the pipes. . . .

CELIA

Can you get your job back?

FATHER

I wish you could see this new place. It's all good hard wood, the dining room's got heavy beams two feet thick, and there's a long oak bar.

CELIA

You could have wired Polo and confirmed the loan before you put any money down . . . certainly before you got men in to go to work.

FATHER

It's not the first time his brother's disappointed me, and look what he's doing now. A bouncer. He calls that place a cocktail lounge? That's no cocktail lounge. I've been in chippie joints in my time, it's more like a cat house. Excuse me, honey, I mean whore house.

JOHNNY

You could have made a two-dollar phone call.

FATHER

For what? Seven months ago when I thought I was going to buy that bar on the Bay, he sent me a check for twenty-five hundred bucks. The deal fell through, and I sent the money back to him. . . . That was seven lousy months ago! The bank never promised me a loan! My son promised me. Now he tells me the money is gone! Gone where? Where did it go?

JOHNNY

Now look, Pop, I know Polo as well as I know myself. If he had the money he'd give it to you.

FATHER

I don't want to be here when he gets back.

JOHNNY

You're not going to hold a grudge against him.

13

CELIA

I'm going to talk to Polo when he comes home.

JOHNNY

Pop, how about some wine?

FATHER

O.K., let's have some wine. Hey, that looks like homemade red.

CELIA

Yes, I buy it from a grocer in the neighborhood.

JOHNNY

He makes it in the cellar. The grocery store is just a front.

FATHER

Hey Johnny, remember the farm we used to have. Remember how we used to hitch those big bay horses to the trees and tear them up by the roots so's we could plant. Look at my hands . . . mixing pink ladies and daiquiris. It's embarrassing.

JOHNNY

What's embarrassing?

FATHER

I have to get a manicure twice a week.

CELIA

I can't imagine Johnny on a farm. He's got a face like the city.

FATHER

Yeh, well, he'd pick tomatoes until he'd fall on his face—walk right under the horse's belly, right, Johnny?

JOHNNY

Right, Pop.

FATHER

I was thinking about getting a farm while you were in the Army, Johnny. Every once in a while now, I feel a funny thing in the air. People look lost to me. All I see is movement. Trains, boats, planes. Look at an oak tree, it doesn't move so that you can notice it. I was thinking about a farm again. I just had the feeling that the time had come to stop . . . and really add up what counts. Maybe look back and see if we didn't pass something by.

CELIA

That's a lovely thought . . .

15

FATHER

Ah . . . It's all talk. When you come right down to it. Nothing is right. Nothing is wrong. Nobody's for, and nobody's against. Something happened somewhere along the line!

JOHNNY

Happened to who, Pop? I don't follow you . . .

FATHER

Happened to us, the people.

CELIA

Well, what happened to us?

FATHER

This is the age of the vacuum. The people—they don't believe any more.

CELIA

You know there's a joke now about "*they*." It's said that when you find out who *they* are, you don't need a psychiatrist any more.

FATHER

Now look, young lady—before psychiatrists struck oil, the bartenders did their job. There's no better place to feel the pulse of the nation.

CELIA

I hope the Senate and the rest of the legislators aren't making a survey of the bars.

JOHNNY

Honey, you're getting red in the face.

CELIA

I've heard this before—the age of the vacuum, everybody's waiting—and no one believes. It's been said enough in the last few years. What's the sense of having a child? Another war may come. Look out for the white light when you hear the siren . . . every time I hear this kind of talk my blood boils. . . .

FATHER

You have to be young to get excited. There's an old Italian saying—

CELIA

I'm not interested in old Italian sayings. Just what do you believe in?

FATHER

What do you suggest I believe in? I'm sorry, I'm trying to take you seriously—

CELIA

You have two sons! You have a grandchild coming—some day Polo will have a wife and there'll be more children.

FATHER

Oh Hell, there will always be children.

CELIA

No, there will not! Because people don't believe in staying married any more. If you can't be happy together, why stay together? Johnny has been back two years, and there hasn't been a married couple in this house for over two years. They're all divorced or separated, and they've excused themselves, and granted one another pardons. No, there will not always be children. Not if people go around talking about the age of the vacuum as if it were an indestructible fact.

JOHNNY

Honey! Calm down, you're going to get the neighbors in here.

CELIA

The neighbors should know that too . . . And I don't want to apologize for anything I've said.
(*The hall lights brighten slightly. A figure scurries down the fire escape. Two men appear in the hallway.*)

FATHER

She's all woman, Johnny—all woman. You know, you look just like Johnny's mother did. That light hair, and—

CELIA

I thought she had dark hair, in the pictures Johnny showed me, she—

FATHER

Sure, she had dark hair, but you look just like her.
(*Another figure has scurried down the fire escape. The three men whisper in the hallway; then the figure scurries up the fire escape again. The tall silhouetted man,* MOTHER, *raps him playfully with the umbrella as he goes up. The smaller figure,* APPLES, *knocks gently at the door.*)

JOHNNY
(*Opens the door*)

Hi!

CELIA

Well, tell them to come in, Johnny. Don't have them standing out in the hall.

JOHNNY

Come on in . . .

(MOTHER *and* APPLES *appear and take a few steps into the* *doorway.* MOTHER *is tall, sleekly dressed and wears a pair* *of dark glasses.* APPLES, *at his side, has on a dirty raincoat.* *Both are wet.*)

MOTHER

(*Looking at shoes*)

Our feet are wet, Johnny. We just want to see you for a minute.

JOHNNY

This is my wife—and this is my father.

FATHER

How do you do?

CELIA

I'm sorry I didn't get your names?

FATHER

Take off your glasses and stay a while.

APPLES

I got your floor all dirty. Maybe I'd better wait out in the hall.

MOTHER

Yeh, wait out in the hall. Could you step out for a few minutes, Johnny. Nice meeting you—

(*They both go out and stand out in the hallway, closing the door after them.* JOHNNY *walks to closet, gets out jacket.*)

CELIA

Who are they?

JOHNNY
(*Smiling*)

They're a couple of guys I play poker with. They probably want to borrow a few bucks. . . .

CELIA

I don't care about the floor, tell them to come in.

JOHNNY

Why don't you get the album out and show the old man the pictures you were talking about? I'll be right back. . . .

CELIA

Put your coat on. It's damp.

(JOHNNY *goes out. Lights dim in apartment area and come up in the hallway.*)

JOHNNY

Look, Mother, everything went wrong. I called the clubhouse, I called Ginnino's, I've been trying to get you all day long.

APPLES

Every junkey in the city has been trying to call us. Right, Mother?

MOTHER

That's right. They picked up Alby this afternoon.

APPLES

We been walking in the shadows all day long. We can't stay in one place more than ten minutes.

MOTHER

The lid is all over the city.

APPLES

This is no three-day affair. They're hitting this city like a hurricane. In a week the city's going to be dry.

JOHNNY

I'm thin, Mother.

MOTHER

I'm no doctor, I'm a businessman.

APPLES

You got it for free in the hospital, Johnny, but Mother's no charity ward.

MOTHER

You got it?

JOHNNY

No.

MOTHER

You ain't even got a hunk of it?

JOHNNY

Where can I get it? All of a sudden you start to close in on me. That kind of money isn't easy to get.

(*The third figure,* CHUCH, *comes slowly down the ladder and hangs over* JOHNNY's *head; in the darkness he could pass for an ape.*)

MOTHER

What have you been trying to get us for then?

JOHNNY

My old man came in tonight. He's going to be here for a few days. I wanted you to give me enough to hold me over, until he gets on his plane. As soon as he goes, I'll try to get the money I owe you.

APPLES

How you going to pay? Two dollars a week for the next five years?

MOTHER

You'll get it by tomorrow morning! Every penny of it . . .

JOHNNY

Oh, Mother, you must be crazy. Where am I going to get seven hundred dollars by tomorrow morning?

APPLES

Your wife must have something for a rainy day. . . . Huh?

JOHNNY

What do you expect me to do! Go to my wife and say—

MOTHER

Chuchie! (*Instantly* CHUCH's *arm comes down and wraps it-self around* JOHNNY, *holding him pressed against the fire-escape ladder*) Now you listen to me, you junkey bastard! I don't care how many jokes you told me, or how long I know you. I'd never press you, if they didn't press me. Your eyes can rattle out of your head. Just good faith . . . five hundred, and I'll carry you for the rest. Let him go, Chuchie. . . .

    (CHUCH *lets his arm loose.*)

JOHNNY

What am I going to do for the next few days . . . ?

MOTHER

Riddle arm, that's your problem. (MOTHER *takes a small packet out of his pocket. He holds it up*) Here. Feel it? Give me the weight minus the paper. And what do you have? Not even an ounce . . . one lousy spoon of morphine, and I put my life on the block every time I put it in my pocket. How many times did I bring it to you? They'll give me ten years for carrying that.

JOHNNY

Thanks, Mother. I'll pay you tomorrow.

MOTHER

Look! You need forty dollars a day now. You can't make it working. I don't care how you make it—push the stuff, steal . . .

APPLES

(*Handing* JOHNNY *a gun*)

Here.

JOHNNY

You guys must be crazy. I don't want that.

APPLES

Keep it. It's not loaded.

JOHNNY

No!

MOTHER

Leave it lay on the floor, Apples. Gimme back that packet, Johnny!

JOHNNY

Look, I walked around all day long trying to—(*Suddenly* MOTHER *kicks* JOHNNY *in the groin*) Sshhhh . . . for. Quiet. My old man's here. . . .

CHUCH

His old man's here, Mother . . . his old man's here. Give him a break, willya. Can't you see he's going to curdle?

MOTHER

(*Taking packet*)
His old man's here, and mine's dead. You go over the roof—and we'll meet you by Ginnino's.

CHUCH

Okay.

MOTHER

Five hundred . . . tomorow morning, Johnny.
(MOTHER *and* APPLES *walk out.*)

CHUCH

Johnny, you all right? Look, Johnny, he's not kidding. It's a shame what they did to Willy DeCarlo this afternoon. He didn't even owe as much as you do. He's no good: Mother . . . he'll do everything but kill you. Be a good guy, pick it up—It's not even loaded.

JOHNNY

Chuchie . . . You got anything at all.

CHUCH

No.

JOHNNY

Even half . . .

CHUCH

I ain't got enough for myself.

JOHNNY

When you tried to kick it, and you couldn't stand it—you called me, and I gave you my last drop.

CHUCH

All right. You come by my house later. And, Johnny, don't say nothing about my dog. I mean if the ole lady says anything, just change the subject. My dog fell out the window last night . . .

JOHNNY

All right, Chuch.

CHUCH

He died, Johnny. Right in my arms.
(CHUCH *scurries up the ladder.* JOHNNY *bends down, picks up the gun and puts it in his jacket pocket. The lights dim in the hallway and come up in the apartment area.*)

FATHER

It wasn't a big farm but you could eat and live off it. A cosmetic factory squeezed me on the mortgage. I built that barn and I was the last one to go. Johnny's mother died a short time after and the kid went to live with his Aunt Grace—No, Polo went to live with his Aunt Grace; Johnny went to live with his Uncle Louis. (JOHNNY *has entered*) What did those characters want?

CELIA

I don't like those men . . .

JOHNNY

They're only a couple of guys I play poker with.

FATHER

Who ever heard of seeing people out in the hall? There's a room right here . . .

JOHNNY

Now, what in the world's the trouble—You've never seen them before.

CELIA

I've seen them with that Willy DeCarlo standing on a corner. And I never liked him coming up here either . . . and you never know where he's looking. He just stares in space.

JOHNNY

You don't see him coming around here any more.

CELIA

How much money did you lose?

JOHNNY

Couple of bucks.

CELIA

Should I try to make some more coffee . . . ?

FATHER

No, not for me, thanks. I'd better get back to the hotel. Oh—
I brought a package in. What happened to it?

CELIA

I think I put it with your coat.

FATHER

When your brother comes in, don't say anything to him,
Johnny. It's all water under the bridge. I bought a half a dozen
Oxford shirts down there . . . they're all brand-new . . . I
figured you and your brother could wear them. Put four of them
in your drawer and give him two.

JOHNNY

Here, honey, put three in Polo's drawer . . .

FATHER

Keep four of them for yourself.

CELIA

You come early for dinner tomorrow night . . . and you
come over for breakfast too. . . .

FATHER

I'll get a couple of box seats for the ball game, Johnny.

JOHNNY

He's got a back like a gorilla . . . he dumped Benny Leonard
once . . . Isn't that right, Pop?

FATHER

Yeh, and I swam the English Channel both ways.

CELIA

Watch your step, Pop.
     (*Goes out and starts down the stairs with* FATHER.)

FATHER

See you in the morning, kid.

JOHNNY

Good night, Pop.

FATHER

Heh, Johnny . . . and if I drop my hat crossing the street . . .

JOHNNY

Oh . . . don't bend down to pick it up.

FATHER

(Like an old vaudevillian)

Why not?

JOHNNY

You'll get an assful of taxicab bumpers . . .
(The FATHER *goes.)*

FATHER

(Off)

That's an old standing gag we used to have.
(We hear their voices trail off. JOHNNY *moves to his jacket, takes out the gun, looks about the room and goes to a drawer to hide the gun. He walks to the kitchen, starts to roll up his sleeves without thinking—catches himself and rolls them down. As he begins to remove objects from the table, he notices the shirts his* FATHER *left and throws them into* POLO's *room. For a split second, he stops moving; he throws his head back, blinks his eyes and shakes his head as if to ward off sleep. He goes to the sink and throws water on his face; then he again begins to clear the table, as* CELIA *enters.)*

CELIA

There's no hot water, is there? Aren't we speaking to one another? The clock has stopped again? I guess we're not speaking to one another. Thanks for clearing the table. The cream belongs in the icebox.

JOHNNY

The refrigerator . . .

CELIA

Johnny, I'm sorry about this morning. It's silly, I don't even know what it was that I said now.

JOHNNY

You said I was useless . . . Something like that.

CELIA

Why should you be afraid to tell me that you lost a job? I felt like a fool when I called . . . your boss must have thought I was a fool, too . . . out of work three days and I have to find out by accident . . .

JOHNNY

I ruined a day's work. A whole day's work just botched . . . I don't know how I did it.

CELIA

Ruining a day's work—losing a job is no reason to go into hiding!

JOHNNY

Honey, I didn't lose that job—I was thrown out. I put fifteen shafts into the lathe that day and I undercut every one by twenty lousy thousandths of an inch. It's the fourth job I've lost in six months.

*

CELIA

All right—but this isn't 1929—so you lost four jobs.

JOHNNY

Where do these go?

CELIA

The top shelf.

JOHNNY

Don't start shouting now . . .

CELIA

I haven't even raised my voice . . .

JOHNNY

I know when you're shouting even when you don't raise your voice.

CELIA

Well, they go on the top shelf. The dishes go on the top shelf. The cream belongs in the ice—refrigerator. Your shoes are to be found in the closet . . . your shirts and shorts are in the

34

bottom drawer. And we live at 967 Rivington Street! Let's not do the dishes. Can't we sit down in the front room. Let's just for once, sit down and talk. Come on, put that down.

JOHNNY

All right. Where do you want to sit? Where do I sit?

CELIA

1999127

Can we try to talk . . .

JOHNNY

I thought everything was decided. Do you leave, or do I leave?

CELIA

I thought we had more to talk about than that.

JOHNNY

Well, go ahead, I'm listening.

CELIA

You'll have to do more than listen.

JOHNNY

I can't talk. I just can't seem to talk to people any more.

CELIA

I'm not people. I'm your wife. I married you to live with you. I married you to have your child in me.

JOHNNY

Look, do we have to sit down like we're holding a class. Well—?

CELIA

Well, what about her? Is she rich? Is she pretty?

JOHNNY

I've told you I haven't even shaken hands with another woman since we've been married. And that's four years.

CELIA

One year, Johnny—that's all the marriage we ever had. The first year. I never said this before, I think I'm ashamed of it . . . but there were many times while you were gone, that I just wanted to be near a man. Sometimes I thought I'd go crazy. I just wanted to go out and watch people dance, I never went anywhere, I waited for you . . .

JOHNNY

I didn't go anywhere either. They told me where to go.

CELIA

I can understand how you might . . . Maybe I haven't given you what you want . . . or need. All right—who is she? Why do you have to lie to me?

JOHNNY

I'm not lying.

CELIA

You must think I've been stupid all these months . . . I thought that if I let you go and not say anything . . . I kept saying to myself, you love me and only me . . .

JOHNNY

I love you, and only you.

CELIA

God, I would like to know where you are! I waited for you and you never came home . . . I was here when you left, while you were gone, and I'm here now. Johnny, I spend more time with your brother than I do with you. Polo and I are together every night of the week. He never mentions you and neither do I. We just pretend that you don't exist . . . being lonely at night is nothing new, but last night I was lonely in a different way. I almost threw myself in Polo's arms.

JOHNNY

What are you talking about?

CELIA

We can't go on living like this any more. Not the three of us in one house. . . . Johnny, we used to talk all night long and wake up bleary-eyed. But it didn't matter because we were together. Don't you remember?

JOHNNY

All week-end long too . . . that week-end we spent at the Point. We didn't sleep from Friday to Sunday. . . .

CELIA

And that poor house detective—he thought we weren't married.

JOHNNY

I told you to get out of the sun and you got sunburned.

CELIA

And I told you we shouldn't go out on the rocks . . . You hobbled around for a week with a stubbed toe.

JOHNNY

And you walked around for a week with that white stuff on your nose—you looked like a clown.

CELIA

The old man who climbed out to where we were, and caught us kissing.

JOHNNY

Caught us kissing . . . ? He must have been watching us for five minutes.

CELIA

Well, that's all we were doing.

JOHNNY

You're not remembering that day. . . .

CELIA

I remember that day most of all. . . . It was your week-end, before you went away. All I wanted to do was hold you and never let you go.

JOHNNY

You cried at the train station.

CELIA

I know. But I didn't know where you **were going and how** long you'd be gone. You cried too. . . .

JOHNNY

No, I didn't.

CELIA

I saw you through the window of the train, just as it was pulling out. You were smiling, but you were crying.

JOHNNY

Well—for crissake—you looked like a kid who lost her rag doll . . .

CELIA

And—we weren't just kissing. The old man saw us—

JOHNNY

Playing. The old man saw us playing.

CELIA

Playing . . . well, that's a new word for—Johnny, please love me.

JOHNNY

Love you? I love you more than I can say. Sometimes at night, when you sleep I walk the streets like I'm looking for something, and yet I know all the while what I want is sleeping. It's like I walk the streets looking for you . . . and you're right here.

CELIA

What's the matter?

JOHNNY

Nothing . . .

CELIA

I didn't mean to offend you by touching you . . .

JOHNNY

I'm sorry . . .

CELIA

Were you with her today . . . ?

JOHNNY

Never mind where I was today.

CELIA

Oh, yes, I'm going to mind . . . You walk the streets at night, you go out any time you want and come home any time you want. A day isn't just a day. It's no longer your day or my day—a day belongs to us both. All right, you didn't work to-day, you'll get another job, but what was today? What was your day? Did you take her to a movie or—

41

JOHNNY

This morning you said that the marriage was a bust, that we were on the rocks . . . After you left . . . Did you ever feel like you were going crazy? Ever since I knew the old man was coming up . . . I just can't stop remembering things . . . like all night long I've been hearing that whistle . . . The old man used to whistle like that when he used to call us . . . I was supposed to come right home from school, but I played marbles. Maybe every half-hour he'd whistle . . . I'd be on my knees in the schoolyard, with my immie glove on—you take a woman's gloves and you cut off the fingers . . . so your fingers are free and your knuckles don't bleed in the wintertime . . . and I just kept on playing and the whistle got madder and madder. It starts to get dark and I'd get worried but I wouldn't go home until I won all the marbles . . . and he'd be up on that porch whistling away. I'd cross myself at the door . . . there was a grandmother I had who taught me to cross myself to protect myself from lightning . . . I'd open the door and go in . . . hold up the chamois bag of marbles and I'd say, hey, Pop, I won! Wham! Pow! . . . I'd wind up in the corner saying, Pop, I didn't hear you. I didn't hear you . . .

CELIA

What did you do today? You didn't play marbles today, did you? You weren't home all day because I called here five times if I called once . . .

JOHNNY

I'm trying to tell you what I did today . . .

42

CELIA

You're trying to avoid telling me what you did today.

JOHNNY

I took a train see . . . then I took a bus . . . I went to look at the house I was born in. It's only an hour away . . . but in fifteen years, I've never gone anywhere near that house . . . or that town! I had to go back . . . I can't explain the feeling, but I was ten years old when I left there . . . The way I looked around, they must have thought I was crazy . . . because I kept staring at the old house—I was going to knock at the door and ask the people if I could just look around . . . and then I went to that Saybrook school where I used to hear the old man whistle . . . and those orange fire escapes . . . and ivy still climbing up the walls. Then I took the bus and the train, and I went to meet the old man's plane . . . and we came here.

CELIA

You came here. Not home . . . but here.

JOHNNY

I mean home.

CELIA

You said here . . .

JOHNNY

All right, here, not home. You know, I've lived in a lot of places since I left that town. There was always a table, some cups and some windows . . . and somebody was the boss, somebody to tell you what to do and what not to do, always somebody to slap you down, pep you up, or tell you to use will power . . . there was always a bed. What do I know about a home?

CELIA

Johnny? Johnny! Do you want to run away from here . . . ?

JOHNNY

I want to live here.

CELIA

With me . . .

JOHNNY

Honey, there is no other woman. Look, baby—you don't know how much I need you, how much I love you, sometimes I want to bury myself in you . . .

CELIA

Well, do. . . .

A HATFUL OF RAIN

JOHNNY

Honey—Honey, I've got to go out tonight . . . but, I'm . . .
I love you . . .

CELIA

The rain's stopped. I think I'd better open the windows . . .
everything's so damp in here.
(*We hear rollicking, happy laughter in the hallway, and*
POLO's *voice.*)

POLO

(*Off*)

Hey, boy, hey, Johnny, the walls are crooked.

JOHNNY

Hold on to those walls.

CELIA

Help him before he falls down the stairs.
(JOHNNY *goes out.* POLO *appears, hanging on* JOHNNY's
arm and shoulder. He is quite drunk.)

POLO

Hey, come on . . . we're all going dancing. Hey, Celia, come
on, we're all going dancing. The floors are crooked, Johnny.

CELIA

You ought to be ashamed of yourself.

45

POLO

I'm so drunk I couldn't walk a chalk line.

JOHNNY

Hold on. Let's see if we can get over to that chair.

POLO

I don't know what that would prove . . . if I could walk a chalk line. Leave me alone, Johnny, I'm all right. Come on, lemme alone . . .

JOHNNY

Come on, let's get those clothes off.

POLO

Hey, Johnny, who you going to vote for Miss Rheingold of 1955?

JOHNNY

I haven't made my mind up yet.

POLO

I voted twenty-three times for Miss Woods . . . You think she cares, Johnny? She doesn't care.

46

CELIA

Here . . . drink this.

POLO

Oh, no, honey—I don't want any of that coffee. I'm not *that* drunk. Hey, hey . . . handle those shoes with care. They're Florsheim shoes . . . Hey, hey . . . le's get some good music on . . . hey, Johnny . . . take it easy with that shirt. That's an Arrow shirt. Hey, Celia, le's get some good music on.

CELIA

You get your clothes off and get to bed.

POLO

Aw come on, don't be a party pooper! Hey, Celia, you know there's a lady lives up there by the second-floor fire escape. . . . Every day, she hangs out her clothes—right, Popo . . . Dopo, Mopo. She dreamt she washed her windows in her Maidenform bra. . . . (*Growl*) Rub-a-dub, dub, three men in her tub . . . blow you March sonofabitchin winds blow. . . .

CELIA

I think we should undress you and put you to bed.

POLO

Oh, no, no . . . You're not undressing me. I'm ashamed. I got a big appendix scar. We all got scars. Johnny's got scars all the way down his back, huh? Johnny was fourteen days in a cave . . . all the way down his back. Celia, meet my brother . . . my guests are his guests . . . but his guests aren't my guests. Celia, Johnny's got a heart like a snake.

JOHNNY

All right, you said enough.

POLO

If I ever catch those sonsabitches around here again, Johnny, I'll tear their heads off.

JOHNNY

Shut up. Why don't you shut up?

POLO

I shut up. I'm shut up. I'm like you, Johnny . . . all you ever gave was your rank, your name and your serial number . . . I don't tell the old man.

JOHNNY

Let's forget the old man and get to bed.

POLO

That's right, Johnny. Let's forget the old man . . . let's forget everybody. We don't need anybody. I got . . . Florsheim

shoes . . . Paris belt . . . hey, where's my Paris belt . . . ?
Thanks, Celia . . . You're an angel in disguise.

CELIA

Good night, Polo.

POLO

Don't worry about me. I got everything I need . . . except
a Bond suit. I dreamt I fell asleep in my Bond suit.
(JOHNNY *leads him off; then comes back.*)

JOHNNY

Just a little high, that's all—like Christmas, once a year.

CELIA

I'd better put this on him. He'll freeze to death. (*The moment she goes into the room,* JOHNNY *goes to the drawer, takes
out the gun and puts it in his pocket.* CELIA *stops in the doorway*)
Where are you going?

JOHNNY

Out, I'm going out, I'll take a walk for myself. Oh, no, leave
your coat where it is. I don't want you coming with me . . .

CELIA

Why not . . . ?

JOHNNY

'Cause, I just want to think . . .

CELIA

I won't even talk, I'll just hold on to your arm.

JOHNNY

You *can't* come with me . . . I'll be back.

CELIA

When? Tell me when so I can wait. Tonight, and—tomorrow, at dawn . . . Noon . . . When?

JOHNNY

Don't be mad, willya?

CELIA

Oh, no, no, no. I won't be mad. Do you know that I fell so in love with you all over again tonight? I wanted you. Do you understand what it means to want someone!

JOHNNY

Look, all the things you said tonight about trying—

CELIA

Trying? I've tried . . . if they gave out medals for trying I'd sink right through this floor. And every week, every day you keep slipping away—Why don't you look around you? You worked on the woodwork like a beaver, you built everything . . . but—nothing here belongs to you. This is yours . . . I'm yours . . . Go on tell her she's welcome to you . . .

JOHNNY

It's not another woman. Will you get that out of your mind . . . get it out, I love you . . . and believe me it's not another woman!

CELIA

Then what is it . . . ? This is the last time you'll ever do this to me.

JOHNNY

I'm sorry.

CELIA

Don't stand with one hand on the doorknob like that. You look like Mickey Rooney leaving Boy's Town forever . . .

(JOHNNY *goes out, closing the door sharply behind him. He walks down the hall; at the end of it he stops.* CELIA *has walked away from the door. For a moment, they start to walk toward the door and each other—but they both stop.* JOHNNY *goes down the stairs.*)

The lights dim out

It is about two o'clock in the morning. The lights are dim. In the darkness we see the city beyond—glowing. There is the sound of a dog barking in the distance. The door to POLO's *room opens, and, in the lighted doorway, we see* POLO *standing in shorts. He moves to the sink shakily and begins throwing water down his throat. . . . The lights are flicked on.*

CELIA

Don't do that, Polo! You'll give yourself a stomach cramp.

POLO

I got no choice . . . stomach cramp or I'll die of thirst . . . Where's my pants . . . who robbed my pants? Hey Johnny, where did you put my pants?

CELIA

Johnny went out.

POLO

You're mad at me too, huh?

CELIA

You ought to be ashamed of yourself. Your father was hurt
. . . you almost took the doors off the hinges slamming it.

POLO

He was hurt, huh? His boy Johnny was here so he shouldn't
feel so bad. Nobody said I was a bum, huh? All right, I never
graduated high school . . . What's that make me, a bum?

CELIA

You're jealous . . .

POLO

Why should I be jealous? It's always been the same. It's not
only him. . . it's all my damn relatives. As long as I can remember, always laughing at me . . .

CELIA

You don't like your father very much, do you? Why didn't
you lend your father the money? He said you promised . . .
he said that—

54

POLO

I know what he said—what I said . . . The money's gone. It flew south with the birds. I bet it on one of Ali Khan's horses—gone is gone, any kid knows that. Gone doesn't come back.

CELIA

I only asked a simple question, Polo.

POLO

I'm glad you didn't ask a difficult one. I don't like my father, huh? He comes over to that nightly circus I work in, he tells me it's a joint. People don't come in there to drink, that's what he says—that's bright on his part. There's thirteen whores leaning on the bar and he tells me people don't come in there to drink.

CELIA

What's the matter with you, Polo? I've never seen you like this before.

POLO

I'm drunk, that's all.

CELIA

I can see that you're drunk.

POLO

Well, can't a guy drink just because he likes to drink? Do you have to have a reason to drink?

CELIA

You don't like Johnny any more, do you? Why does he have a heart like a snake?

POLO

You're starting to sound like the 47th Precinct. Why? What? Who?

CELIA

Sometimes I get the feeling that you hate your brother . . .

POLO

I'll tell you one thing, I used to hate him . . . When I was a kid . . . Johnny kept getting adopted, nobody ever adopted me. *And I wanted to get adopted.* They'd line us up, and he'd get picked—then he'd run away and come back to the home the old man put us in . . . and I used to think to myself . . . just let me get adopted once and I'll stay. I used to hate him every time he left—and every time he came back. He'd say the same goddamn thing . . . We gotta stick together, Polo . . . we're the only family we got.

CELIA

Johnny never told me that . . .

POLO

Johnny never told you a lot of things. What I mean is . . . it's not a nice thing to say about the old man, is it?

CELIA

Polo, I want you to tell me what the matter is!

POLO

Why don't you ask your husband Johnny what's the matter with him and leave me alone?

CELIA

Everybody wants to be left alone. We're getting to be a house full of Garbos.

POLO

Just leave me alone . . .

CELIA

Just like Johnny. If I closed my eyes, I'd think you were Johnny.

POLO

You ask the old man who I am, he'll tell you. I'm Polo, the no-good sonofabitch. He'll never forget anything. I threw a lemon at a passing car once . . . and hit the driver in the head. I set fire to a barn once . . . and I never graduated high school. No, I'm not Johnny, he's my brother and he's a sonofabitch. That sonofabitch is going to kill me.

(CELIA *throws a glass of water in* POLO's *face.*)

CELIA

I'm sorry I did that.

POLO

It's a sign of the times . . . a sign of the times. All the king's men, and all the king's horses . . . Oh, what's the difference. (*He goes into his room.*)

CELIA

Polo? Polo? Will you come out and talk to me.

POLO

No!

CELIA

Polo, please, I'm lonely.
(POLO *comes out.*)

58

CELIA

There's some muffins from tonight's supper. Would you like
one?

POLO

No.

CELIA

Well, I'm going to have one.

POLO

I'll have one too. How's the job . . . ?

CELIA

Johnny got fired.

POLO

I know Johnny got fired. I was asking about your job.

CELIA

Well, why didn't you come and tell me that, Polo?

POLO

Honey, I'm not a personnel manager, I'm just a boarder.

CELIA

You're a bouncer in a cat house . . .

POLO

Who said that?

CELIA

Your father . . .

POLO

There must have been a full moon last night . . . boy, they showed up last night, mean, ugly and out of their minds . . . That slap-happy bouncer I work with, if he'd just learn to try to talk these bums out of the place—he's always grabbing somebody by the seat of their pants, and we're off. You know that sonofabitchin bouncer is six foot three and, as God is my witness, honey, every time hell breaks loose I'm in there getting the hell kicked out of me and that big bastard is up against the wall cheering me on! Atta boy, Polo! Atta boy! You got him going. Who have I got going? Who? I'll be punchy before Christmas.

CELIA

You're too light to be a bouncer, Polo. Why don't you quit?

POLO

Quit? Where can I make a hundred and twenty-five dollars a week? Where? Well, you can't beat it. You come into the world poor and you go out owing money. . . .

60

CELIA

You can say that again. . . .

POLO

You come into the world poor, and . . .

CELIA

All right, smarty, forget it. . . . The Union Metal Company of America . . . that's where you should work, Polo. At least there's a little excitement at your job . . . Do you know that when I started working in the carpeted air-conditioned desert I could take dictation at the rate of 120 words a minute? I could type ninety words . . . Today I was sitting at my desk, pretending to be busy. I have papers in all the drawers. I keep shuffling them from drawer to drawer. I break pencils and sharpen them. Mr. Wagner called me in his office today and I bustled in with my steno pad and . . . you know what he called me in for? He wanted to know. Was I happy? Was Union Metals treating me right? I've been there five years come Ash Wednesday . . . and every six months they call you in and ask you the same thing. . . . Are you happy?

POLO

Why don't you quit?

CELIA

Nobody ever quits Union Metals . . . and no one ever gets fired. A bonus on Christmas, a turkey on Thanksgiving, long holiday week-ends. They've insured Johnny and I against sickness, and the plague, everything for the employees . . . boat rides, picnics, sick leave, a triple-savings interest, the vacations keep getting longer, we have a doctor, a nurse, and a cafeteria, four coffee breaks a day, if it gets too hot they send you home, and if it rains it's perfectly all right if you're late . . . and it's the dullest job in the whole world.

POLO

Honey . . . you know what? You've got a real problem there.

CELIA

I don't know whether to laugh or cry. . . .

POLO

Why?

CELIA

I got another raise today. . . .

POLO

Boy, I wish I didn't know right from wrong . . .

CELIA

What?

POLO

Nothing. . . .

CELIA

Polo, I've been wanting to talk to you every night this week.

POLO

We've been here every night this week . . . That's all we've done is talked.

CELIA

You're not listening to me, Polo. I've always liked you and Johnny thinks the world of you, but . . . but . . . I'm afraid you'll have to find a different place to live. . . . Maybe you could take a room somewhere in the neighborhood and still come over to dinner.

POLO

I could, huh? And what about breakfast . . . ?

CELIA

You could come over for breakfast too . . . And I could do your shirts and everything but you'll have to find a different place to live.

POLO

I can do my own shirts . . . Why do I have to move?

CELIA

I know how you feel about me and it's embarrassing.

POLO

Love shouldn't be embarrassing.

CELIA

It's not really embarrassing, but I don't think the three of us can live together any more. I want you out of this house to-morrow. Tomorrow night—after dinner, your father gets his plane. I want you to leave.

POLO

Why?

CELIA

Because I don't want to take any chances.

POLO

What chances?

CELIA

Polo, let's not be children. You do know the difference be-tween right and wrong and so do I. Tomorrow . . . I don't want you to go, but you have to. . . .

POLO

Tomorrow, for crissakes, even Simon Legree gave Little Eva two weeks' notice.

CELIA

I'm going to bed.

POLO

Yeh, go to bed. You're tired. Lay your head down on the pillow and close your eyes. If you want me to go, I'll go, but tonight I'll be in the room next to yours . . . I'll say I love you, but you won't be able to hear me because you'll be asleep. Maybe I'll sing you a lullaby.

CELIA

Polo, why are you doing this? Why now? We've been to-gether so many nights and you've never been like this. . . . Why?

POLO

I'm drunk, that's the prize excuse for anything. I'm drunk and I don't know what I'm saying or doing. I could never say anything if I was sober . . . Celia?

CELIA

What?

65

POLO

Look, you know how I feel about you. How do you feel about me?

CELIA

I don't know.

POLO

Let's feel and find out.

CELIA

Please . . . don't.

POLO

Why didn't you slap me! I'll bet I could kiss you again and you wouldn't raise your hand.

CELIA

Why don't you? Go ahead, don't stop . . . pick me up in your arms and carry me to your brother's bed; I'm going to have a baby, Polo, so I might be a little heavy.

POLO

I'm sorry, but I love you. I didn't ask to. I didn't want to, but I do.

CELIA

Johnny . . . please go to bed.

POLO

I'm not Johnny, I'm Polo. . . .

Curtain

ACT TWO

ACT TWO

Scene I

It is about eight o'clock the following morning. CELIA *is in the kitchen and* POLO *in his bedroom.*

CELIA

Polo, your coffee's poured. Polo? Are you up?

POLO

I'm up.

CELIA

On your feet? I've called you three times.

POLO

All right. (*A moment later* POLO *appears in the doorway. He is wearing pajamas that are three sizes too big for him*) Good morning.

CELIA

Good morning . . . Those pajamas? They're big enough for two people.
    (*Rolling up his sleeve.*)

71

POLO

Christmas present. My relatives.

CELIA

They're absolutely precious. . . . I'm sorry, Polo, but they're hysterical.

POLO

Honey, what do you put in this coffee?

CELIA

Coffee and water and don't kid me about my coffee.

POLO

Well, for crissakes, do you know it has to boil?

CELIA

Give it back. I'll let it boil.

CELIA

See that Johnny gets these things for supper. I think you *should* come to supper and apologize to your father.

POLO

Since when do you have to apologize because you don't have money. If it's all the same to you I'll stop in Nedicks. They're running a special this week, two skinless franks and all the orange juice you can drink.

CELIA

You'll come to supper tonight.

POLO

Who said so?

CELIA

I said so.

POLO

I'll come to supper tonight. Boy, you're really going this morning. Did you have a long talk with God last night? You're like a new washing machine—pa ta-poom, pa ta-poom.

CELIA

You know what? You're blushing. Is your head killing you?

POLO

It isn't bleeding, is it?

CELIA

You're red as a beet.

POLO

I said an awful lot last night. I'm sorry. . . . I'm not sorry, I just think I should say I'm sorry. Just roll the sleeve up. Don't sit in my lap.

CELIA

I wasn't going to sit in your lap, Polo. What's so funny?

POLO

Nothing. I'm just so tired I'm silly. Did you ever get that tired? I'm so tired that nothing matters. I think if you dropped dead right now I'd laugh.

CELIA

That's sweet.

POLO

Where is Johnny?

CELIA

I don't know.

POLO

Well, where is he? Isn't that any of your business? I'll tell you the truth, sometimes . . . you just get me sick. He's your husband, isn't he? He hasn't been home all night . . . that happens two, three times a week. Honest it's been like living in a nut house.

CELIA

Polo! Johnny never asked me whether it would be all right if you came here and lived with us. He said you needed a home and brought you here.

74

POLO

I'm getting out. When I get good and ready and not before. I paid my rent this week.

CELIA

All right.

POLO

You see, you're like a dishrag. I thought I had to get out to-night—you didn't want to take any chances. Why don't you stand up on your feet!

CELIA

I've been standing on my feet all night long, Polo.

POLO

I must be going out of my mind. I could of sworn that I heard you come to my door . . . like a mirage, you want something and you see it . . . even when it's not there.

CELIA

Would you ask Johnny to take the laundry out when he comes in?

POLO

I'll take it out.

CELIA

Let Johnny do it.

POLO

All right! I'll let Johnny do it!

CELIA

There's no need to shout at me, Polo!

POLO

No, huh . . . You don't think so. For six months I kept my peace . . . You had your life to live and I let you live it, but I'm so in love with you . . . that I don't know what to do. But I'm just so fed up watching you being thrown away—What'll I do, go to Alaska—join the Foreign Legion? All right, I love you and I'll get out of here as soon as I can. Now leave me alone! And if my sleeves roll down, just keep your hands off me. . . . I'll roll them up myself.

CELIA

Now you shut up!

POLO

Boy, that's getting to be a habit with you.

CELIA

I don't need you to tell me what I've been doing or what I haven't been doing.

POLO

Then you tell me. Why don't you ask—where he is? Where has he been? What has he been doing? How do you stand it day in and day out. Don't you want to know where your kid's going to live. You're going to have a baby, how do you live a life turning your back on what's been happening? You tell me.

CELIA

Because I don't love Johnny.

POLO

That's not true.

CELIA

It is—I don't love him.

POLO

All right.

CELIA

He hasn't even so much as held my hands in months. When he comes home at night, when he comes home, I pretend I'm sleeping . . . you'd think he'd touch my back, or kiss me good night. He wouldn't know the difference if he found Santa Claus in bed. He doesn't talk, he's always going . . . I'm having a baby, his baby and he never mentions the child or anything about it. Like anyone else . . . I need. Love, children . . . a

77

home. He used to be like you . . . but he's not any more, and it's too late . . . it's too late.

POLO

We're all nice people. . . . Come on, now, stop crying.

CELIA

I can't tell him.

POLO

Why not?

CELIA

I don't know. I don't even know who he is. He's a stranger . . . I never married that person. . . . I thought he was so full of love. I don't know what it is . . . but it doesn't matter any more because I don't love him, and I can't tell him that.

POLO

Listen, are you sure? Maybe you're—maybe you just want to get even, show him something.

CELIA

Last night—and it wasn't a mirage, Polo—That was me at your door.

POLO

But you couldn't come in the door—and I couldn't open it.

CELIA

You take the laundry out.

POLO

Do you think I could . . . just put my arms around you? Do you think it would be all right?

CELIA

I think so.

POLO

When will you tell him?

CELIA

Tonight. You'll be here tonight?

POLO

Yes.

CELIA

Have the laundry bleached and dried.

POLO

All right.

CELIA

I don't want to go to work.

79

POLO

You'd better.

CELIA

I think I'd better. When he comes home, make him take a bath and put on his flannel pajamas.

The lights dim out

Scene II

It is about ten in the morning. As the lights dim up, JOHNNY *is seen coming down the fire escape. Halfway down, he slips; panicked, he grabs the railing and stops his fall. He steadies himself and then climbs down to the hall. He opens the door and enters the kitchen. The door to* POLO's *room is ajar.*

JOHNNY

Polo! Hi!

POLO

Welcome home.

JOHNNY

Celia go to work?

POLO

It's ten o'clock in the morning. She starts at nine . . . she's not here, so figure it out for yourself.

JOHNNY

The old man wanted you to have those shirts. How do they fit?

81

POLO

I haven't put it on yet.

JOHNNY

I was out all night.

POLO

No kidding. Your wife wants you to get these things for supper.

JOHNNY

Where you going?

POLO

I'm going to take the laundry out. . . .

JOHNNY

You know what's happening . . .

POLO

I read the papers. Where you been?

JOHNNY

All over.

POLO

Where's all over?

JOHNNY

All over . . . Harlem, Lower East Side . . . everybody's disappeared.

POLO

It'll all blow over in a few weeks. . . .

JOHNNY

No. No . . . they dropped the net, Polo . . . they're starting to tie the knot. Every pusher in the city's vanished. . . . Look, Polo. . . . I was lucky. I met Ginnino. I told him to hold some for me . . . I have to get to him in fifteen minutes.

POLO

Who fixed you last night?

JOHNNY

Chuchie . . . I stopped over his place. He gave me half of his . . . enough to carry me through the night . . . but I'm thin now, Polo.

POLO

I told you yesterday, Johnny, the cupboard's bare. I'm out of the box and that's all there is to it. If I inherited the Chrysler building right now I wouldn't give you another dime. Try to understand that.

JOHNNY

Don't start lecturing me now. All I need is twenty bucks—and he won't do business on credit.

POLO

Take the kitchen set down and sell it to the Salvation Army. This linoleum isn't in bad shape. If you sell it at night in the dark, maybe you can get a few bucks for it. . . .

JOHNNY

Polo, you know I never sold a thing out of this house and I never will.

POLO

Try to listen, Johnny, try to hear me. I felt great refusing the old man that twenty-five hundred because I know the money went to a good cause. . . . It's only something he wanted all his life. You were right in the middle when he shouted, "Where? Where did it go?"

JOHNNY

Yeh, I was right in the middle. And I almost said, "Here!" It went here.

(*Thrusting his arm forward.*)

POLO

You went through that twenty-five hundred like grease through a tin horn. . . . I'm afraid to park my car out front . . . you might steal it some night.

84

JOHNNY

I'm quitting tomorrow. Tomorrow I'm quitting. . . .

POLO

It's been tomorrow for months, Johnny, the calendar never moves.

JOHNNY

Polo! This is the last time I'll ask you . . . I need twenty bucks. . . .

POLO

Twenty bucks, twice a day.

JOHNNY

Where am I gonna get it?

POLO

Get yourself a black felt hat, cut holes in it for eyes, and go down in the men's room of the subway like Apples does and clobber some poor bastard over the head. . . .

JOHNNY

The answer is no?

POLO

You look tired. . . .

JOHNNY

Here. . . . (*Tosses gun on bed*) I almost used it four times last night . . . I picked dark streets and I waited. Four times . . . and they were set-ups. An old guy . . . must have been eighty years old . . . all alone. A guy and his girl, a young kid coming home from a dance drunk . . . some woman. Four times I left the doorway—I was on top of them . . . They weren't even afraid of me. I asked for a match, which way Fifty-sixth Street was . . . and would you give me a light please. Dust—that's all. Tired feet, tired eyes, and jammed up log tight.

POLO

Where did you get this . . . ?

JOHNNY

The lousy bastards told me it wasn't loaded. I'm into them for seven or eight hundred . . . on top of your twenty-five hundred cash. They want their money today . . . They'll be coming for me.

POLO

What do you mean?

JOHNNY

What do you think I mean?

86

POLO

It's not going to be Mother and Apples alone . . . they know I'm here, they'll bring company. Put those shoes on and let's get out of here.

JOHNNY

No more running, Polo. I'm through running. I can't run any more. If they don't get me today, they'll get me tomorrow.

POLO

You saw what happened to Willy DeCarlo . . .

JOHNNY

I'm not running away from them . . . and that's that! I'm going to stay right here. . . .

POLO

You're crazy, you're going crazy!

JOHNNY

I'm not moving. . . .

POLO

I haven't got seven or eight hundred dollars, Johnny . . . there's nothing I can do.

JOHNNY

Take the laundry out . . . and go to a movie or something.

POLO

What are you going to do?

JOHNNY

I'm going to wait for them . . .

POLO

You going to fight back . . . ?

JOHNNY

Well, I'm not going to stand still while they beat the hell out
of me. . . .

POLO

You can't win . . . they'll kick your ribs in.
(FATHER *knocks and enters.*)

JOHNNY

Hi ya, Pop, you're up early . . .

FATHER

Good morning, Johnny—

POLO

Good morning, Pop. . . . I said good morning, Pop . . .

FATHER

Good morning.

POLO

I'm sorry about last night—

FATHER

How's the boy, Johnny . . . ?

POLO

I'm sorry about not getting to dinner last night . . . Pop, I got looped. Come on, Pop, how about shaking hands and turning over a new leaf . . .

FATHER

I made a long-distance call to Palm Beach this morning trying to get the carpenter . . . and the plumber but I can't. They're putting in eight hours today, maybe copper tubing behind the bar . . .

JOHNNY

Have you had your breakfast—maybe I can whip you up a few scrambled. . . .

FATHER

I'll bet I could throw dollar bills out that window all morning long and there wouldn't be enough on the sidewalk to pay off the money I'm losing today. . . .

JOHNNY

We got an electric orange-juice squeezer—how about if I squeeze up some juice . . .

FATHER

I'm renovating a building I'll never be able to buy . . .

POLO

I'm sorry, Pop. I said I was sorry and I mean it.

FATHER

You said a lot of other things.

POLO

Let's shake hands on it, what do you say?

JOHNNY

The kid's got his hand out waiting for yours. . . .

POLO

I'd like to go to that ball game with you, Pop. Today's my day off . . .

FATHER

You made a jackass out of me! They'll laugh at me down there. I tell all my friends about you kids . . .

JOHNNY

Take the laundry out . . .

POLO

For crissakes, Pop, I haven't got the money. I'm not holding out on you.

JOHNNY

Take the laundry out!

POLO

I don't want to take it out.

JOHNNY

Take it out.

POLO

All right, Johnny.
 (*He goes out.*)

FATHER

A good rain cleans the streets . . . huh?

JOHNNY

You're up early, Pop.

FATHER

I didn't get much sleep. I was wondering about something, Johnny. Is today your day off? I mean, how can you take in the ball game if you're working?

JOHNNY

I'm not working.

FATHER

You say you and your wife are getting along . . . ?

JOHNNY

Yeh . . .

FATHER

Last night, when I went back to the hotel, I kept thinking about what your wife said, about believing. About what do I believe in. She's right, I got you kids to believe in. Like I come up here—you got a wife, a little home, a kid on the way, you're making a home for your brother. You did a good job of bringing yourself up . . . but what the hell's your brother doing? Holing up in some dame's apartment? Twenty-five hundred is a—

JOHNNY

I don't know. . . .

FATHER

You talk in awful short phrases, Johnny. . . .

JOHNNY

I'm not too used to talking to you, Pop.

FATHER

That's right, we don't talk very much, do we?

JOHNNY

No. . . .

FATHER

I like the letters you write me, Johnny . . . Life plays funny tricks on people. Hello and Good-bye . . . and nothing in between, but I like the letters you write me.

JOHNNY

I'm glad you do, Pop.

FATHER

You take this believing thing—after your mother died, I used to read to you and your brother . . . Hi Diddle Diddle, the Cat and the Fiddle, Easter Bunny, Santa Claus and all that crap. You'd believe everything. I'd tell Polo Santa Claus was coming, and he'd look at me like I was out of my mind. You understand what I mean . . . ?

JOHNNY

I'm trying to, Pop. . . .

FATHER

Well, some people can talk, they have all the words. There are some things I feel that I don't have the words for. Maybe you're a little bit like me because you don't seem to be able to talk to me. . . .

JOHNNY

I always wanted to talk to you, Pop, but it's like you never wanted to talk to me, like you were afraid . . .

FATHER

What I want to say is that I care what happens to you. . . .

JOHNNY

Thanks. . . .

FATHER

And I love you—that's the thing, see?

JOHNNY

You what?

FATHER

You heard me the first time. Don't make me say it again.

JOHNNY

I feel the same way, Pop—

FATHER

How's that?

JOHNNY

You know what I mean—Polo, you and me, we're all kinda
—Pop, willya do something for me. I never asked you for anything. When the kid comes back, tell him it's all water under the
bridge. . . . Oh. . . .

FATHER

What's the matter?

JOHNNY

Headache . . .

FATHER

You wouldn't know anything about what happened to that
money. Or would you? He doesn't pay a hundred dollars a
week board here, does he?

JOHNNY

I'm asking you for something now. When Polo comes—

FATHER

That's the difference between you and Polo, you never asked
me for anything.

JOHNNY

He never asked you for anything either, Pop.

FATHER

Yeh, but the way he looked at me sometimes—Maybe I never gave you much either.

JOHNNY

You gave me a coat once!

FATHER

A coat?

JOHNNY

Yeh, you came to the home, and you took me out to a department store—and you let me pick out a coat. And then you took me to a restaurant and made the guy give me some wine. . . .

FATHER

Your brother doesn't gamble, does he?

JOHNNY

No. . . .

FATHER

I always kinda thought that you and your brother and I had a special thing. I thought we were just kinda three men . . . Your brother did a lot of shouting last night.

JOHNNY

Pop, you did a little shouting yourself last night.

FATHER

I lived with my father until I was twenty-two years old, and I never raised my voice above a whisper . . .

JOHNNY

He lived with his father for nine years. What did you expect, Little Lord Fauntleroy.

FATHER

I expect the same thing I get from you. You don't go around crying like a kid in a crib. I like the letters you write me—'cause they're a man's letter. Dammit, you had a tough life but you made the best of it. Ever since he left home . . .

JOHNNY

He didn't leave home. He was sent away. Every time he gets a letter from you, he goes into his room and reads it. He's got a box of them in there. . . .

FATHER

Yeh . . . ?

JOHNNY

Yeh.

FATHER

Well, how would I know that!

JOHNNY

He's missed you for a long time, Pop. You shipped him out to uncles and aunts . . .

FATHER

And what was I doing? Gambling, drinking, laying on my can in Bermuda. I don't know anything about him. . . .

JOHNNY

Well, when he comes in, you ask him about that time in the orphan home when he wet the bed, and they made him stand on a staircase all day long with the wet sheet over his head . . .

FATHER

I shipped him—What was I supposed to do, buy a house, work nights, wash clothes during the day? Uncles and aunts, thank God he had them . . .

JOHNNY

All right, Pop . . .

FATHER

A man has only two hands.

JOHNNY

All right, Pop . . .

FATHER

And don't go around all-righting me. When I came yesterday, I had a funny feeling. Right now I got it again. You're not glad to see me, are you?

JOHNNY

Pop, I don't want to talk about it.

FATHER

You're not glad to see me, are you?

JOHNNY

Nobody's blaming you for anything. . . .

FATHER

You both always had a roof over your heads.

JOHNNY

Yeh, but when we woke up we didn't know what roof we were under.

FATHER

Waking up in a hotel room is no fun . . .

JOHNNY

Nobody's blaming you. When you stand in the snow your feet get cold—if you fall in the water and you can't swim, you drown. We call you Pop, and you call us Son, but it never was . . .

FATHER

You're a pretty cold-hearted cookie, Johnny.

JOHNNY

I don't save your letters . . . and I never saved my money to try to help you out. Don't come around knocking Polo to me . . . because he's my brother.

FATHER

And I'm not your father?

JOHNNY

Don't put words in my mouth . . .

FATHER

What the hell's the matter with you—all the things you say? What are you—the lawyer in the case . . . !

JOHNNY

I know you, Pop—either you clam up, or you start to push . . .

FATHER

As I listen to you, it sounds like I don't even know you. . . .

JOHNNY

Don't start to steam!

FATHER

I don't even know you!

JOHNNY

All right, you don't even know me.

FATHER

I don't even know you!

JOHNNY

How the hell could you know me? The last time I saw you I was in the hospital. You came to see me for three days. Before that . . . I saw you for two days, when I graduated school. How the hell could you know me? When you came to the hospital . . . you said, Jesus, it must have been rough, kid but it's all over . . . that's all you had to say . . . we shook hands, like two big men.

FATHER

If you felt that was wrong, why didn't you tell me.

JOHNNY

Tell you what? All I remember is laying there and smiling, thinking the old man's come to take me home.

FATHER

I live in a hotel, Johnny!

JOHNNY

Two big days. Six lousy visiting hours, and you run out. I was so glad to see you. . . .

FATHER

Your wife was there to take you home.

JOHNNY

I knew my wife for one year. I've known you for twenty-seven. Twenty-seven years. Your son! My boy Johnny. I didn't even know who she was.

(POLO *enters.*)

FATHER

That's a helluva thing to tell me—you didn't know who your wife was. You're not gonna blame me, are you? What's the matter with your brother?

POLO

Come on, Johnny, sit down. Sit down, will you.

JOHNNY

No, no, come on, let me stand up. I'd like to tell you right now what's standing in front of you . . . and it's not your Johnny boy.

POLO

No, Johnny, don't!

JOHNNY

I told you about the Sergeant, Polo. I told you all about that sonofabitchin Sergeant.

POLO

Come on, Pop, take a walk.
> (JOHNNY *is not only disturbed by the pent-up emotion, but the narcotic's absence is beginning to become physically apparent.*)

JOHNNY

Tell him what they give you, Polo, tell him. He walked out, like the Sergeant ran out . . . The nurse came, and the doctor . . . They roll up your sleeve—one—then two—then another. You know what I'm talking about? Your son's trying to tell you something. . . .

FATHER

What have you been doing—hitting cheap gin?

POLO

You'd better go, Pop.

JOHNNY

And you come around here talking about an oak tree.

103

FATHER

Don't shake your finger in my face . . .

JOHNNY

I'm trying to tell you something, old man. . . .

POLO

Johnny, lay off . . .

FATHER

Are we still going to have supper tonight?

JOHNNY

Sure, we're going to have supper tonight. Why not?

FATHER

Why don't you meet me at the hotel in an hour or so? We'll
go up and see the ball game.

POLO

Johnny and I will both be there. . . .

FATHER

You better see that he gets to bed. Make him get some sleep.
(*The* FATHER *moves into the hallway.* POLO *follows him.*)

POLO

He's not feeling good, Pop. He doesn't mean—

FATHER

He means it, Polo.

JOHNNY

Okay, Sergeant. It's okay. Every man for himself. It's okay, Sarge. I got your number.

POLO
(Off)

I'll see you in an hour. . . . (*Returning*) Come, Johnny, on your feet and walk around. Come on, get up. Take your shirt off, you're starting to sweat.

JOHNNY

Close the window, it's cold.

POLO

Johnny, I'm going to turn you in. (*Moves to phone*) Johnny? Tell me to pick it up. Nobody will hate you, tell me to pick it up, will you?

JOHNNY

Tomorrow. Don't touch that . . . don't touch it, Sarge. Look, we'll get out of here alive.

POLO

Johnny! Johnny. This is Polo.

JOHNNY

The Sergeant—where's the Sergeant?

POLO

He's not here.

JOHNNY

You don't know what it is to need something, Sergeant. All alone in a cave and not a crumb in the whole cave.

POLO

Johnny, get up!

JOHNNY

You're not going to leave me, Sergeant.

POLO

No, Johnny. I'm not going to leave you. Come on get up. Now slow, go slow, Johnny.

JOHNNY

I'm all right, I'm all right. You go to sleep, Sarge. I'll watch for you. . . . Twenty dollars, that's all I need. Twenty dollars and I'll be the night watchman. . . . Twenty dollars, Sarge.

106

I'll go to the desk myself. I'll turn myself in. (POLO *is at the phone*) What are you doing with that? What are you taking my goddamn shoes for? You leave me something to eat, 'ya hear! (JOHNNY *grabs the phone*) What are you taking my shoes for?

POLO

Johnny, give me the phone.

JOHNNY

You're not going to leave me, Sergeant, are you? Don't leave me, all I need is twenty lousy bucks.

POLO

Twenty bucks twice a day.

JOHNNY

Leave me something to eat, you hear? Go ahead, run! Run! Run and leave me alone, you sonofabitch. I can't move but you run, run and leave me here to die by myself, you sonofabitch.

POLO

Johnny!

JOHNNY

Sssssshhhh. Quiet. Be quiet. Here they come, run for it, run for it. Oh God, here they come. Hit it! Hit it!
(*He cowers on the bed.*)

POLO

For the love of God, Johnny, it's Polo. . . . It's your brother. It's Polo. . . . Polo!

JOHNNY

Hit me, go ahead. Hit me. I don't have to tell you anything. There was nobody here with me. Nobody. Corporal John Pope, 122036617. Name, rank, serial number. I don't know who took my shoes.

(MOTHER *and* APPLES *appear.*)

POLO

Come on, will you snap out of it. Mother, do something for him. I'll make good for it.

MOTHER

I'd like to laugh, but I can't. The pocket's in trouble.

JOHNNY

Go ahead, beat me. I'm bleeding, but beat me. You sonsa-bitches—go ahead! Watch my back—will you watch my back —beat me, 1220—122036617—John Pope.

POLO

Give him something to quiet him down. I'll make good for it.

APPLES

He must think you're the Chase National Bank, Mother. We don't wake up and find our money in a rain barrel.

POLO

On my word of honor, I'll pay you tomorrow.

MOTHER

All eight hundred. You got enough to cover this trip.

POLO

I swore if it killed me I wasn't going to put another nickel into that arm!

JOHNNY

Don't hit me—will you watch my back. I didn't have a gun. I don't know who took my shoes.

POLO

Take it. You're the Mother of them all. Go ahead, count it.

APPLES

Mother's got a Horn and Hardart mentality. Nickels and dimes, right, Mother. Right?

MOTHER

I'll tell you what I'm going to do. I'll set him straight for twelve bucks. . . . We'll give him back his spine. Then we're going to work him over.

POLO

You'll get yours someday, Mother. I'll see that you get paid in full someday.

JOHNNY

122036617! That's all I have to tell you. Nobody with me . . . that's all.

MOTHER

(*Picking up* JOHNNY)
Just take it easy, Corporal—the General's here.

JOHNNY

(*As he is carried out by* MOTHER)
Watch my back. . . . Watch my back.

APPLES

Old Mother's got some sense of humor—the General's here. You shouldn't treat Mother like a smell. You know the British Government's been sending tax collectors into the bush for years . . . trying to get them pygmy bastards to pay up their back taxes. That's right. Flies don't have brains . . . and pygmies don't have money, but they got goats. They got to pay their back taxes with goats . . . you understand. Flies don't have brains, but he's got brains.
(MOTHER *has returned*.)

MOTHER

You don't need a car in the city, no place to park.

APPLES

Allus getting parkin' tickets . . .

MOTHER

You got your keys . . . ?

POLO

Yeh.

MOTHER

You got your pink slip?

POLO

Yeh.

MOTHER

You get to the nearest used-car lot and sell that car! I want eight hundred dollars. We'll be back tonight. We don't get that money—we put your brother in the hospital with Willy De-Carlo. . . . Maybe we send you along too. Let's move it!
    (*He and* APPLES *leave.*)

JOHNNY

        (*Comes into the kitchen*)
Where'd they go?

POLO

Are you all right?

111

JOHNNY

I'm all right. Polo—

POLO

Johnny— The shopping list is on the table, Johnny. I got something to do before I meet the old man. Do you want us to pick you up . . . go to the game with us?

JOHNNY

No, I think I'd better stay here.

POLO

I'll see you at supper.

JOHNNY

Polo . . . I have to tell her, but what can I say? I don't know what the hell's happening to me . . . that's the trouble . . . yesterday, I went all the way over to that Summittown . . . and I stand there like an idiot looking at the house. It's all gone, what the hell am I looking for? I trust you, Polo—how can I tell her?

POLO

Tell her, Johnny, just tell her.

JOHNNY

What'll I say for crissakes?

POLO

Just say . . . uh . . . I'm a junkey. That's what you are, isn't it, Johnny?

The lights dim out

Scene III

It is early the same evening. As the lights fade in, we hear faintly the music of a street carousel and the eager, happy voices of children in the street below. Odd fragments of the phrases, "Ma, Ma, I wanna go again. . . ." JOHNNY, *wearing a neatly pressed shirt, is in the kitchen, spreading a tablecloth. He moves to the sink, and, as he turns around, we see that he has a bouquet of flowers; he sets them on the table. As he hears* CELIA *approach, he moves hurriedly into* POLO'S *room, leaving the door ajar.* CELIA *enters.*

CELIA

Polo.

JOHNNY
(*From within*)

Yeh.

CELIA

Did Johnny go to the game?

JOHNNY
(*Still inside*)

Yeh.

114

CELIA

The flowers are beautiful. What smells so good? What are you doing in there? The kids are riding the carousel. The old horse looks like he wants to go home and sleep. (JOHNNY *sneaks up behind her and puts his hands over her eyes*) What are you doing? A surprise . . . what's the surprise?

JOHNNY

Me.

CELIA

I thought you were going to the game with your father.

JOHNNY

Let's go down and ride the carousel.

CELIA

I've got to get things ready. Did Polo go to the game?

JOHNNY

Yeh. Come on, let's go down and take one ride on it.

CELIA

We'd break the horses.

JOHNNY

How was your day?

115

CELIA

What?

JOHNNY

I said, how was your day?

CELIA

Like any other day. Why?

JOHNNY

Why? I thought you said that a day wasn't just a day.

CELIA

Oh. I'll have to make a salad.

JOHNNY

It's in the icebox.

CELIA

I'll have to make the dressing.

JOHNNY

It's in the blue cup. I've looked for the shoe polish all day and I can't find it. Where do you hide it?

CELIA

The cabinet . . . under the sink. You did the floors.

JOHNNY

I swished a mop around. I took all my clothes to the cleaners, and I fixed that clock.

CELIA

You didn't look for a job today, did you?

JOHNNY

No, I didn't have time.

CELIA

I didn't mean anything. I was just curious . . . that's all.

JOHNNY

Yeh. You want to sit in a tub of hot water . . . I'll rub your back with alcohol.

CELIA

What is this? Flowers, the floors mopped, meat in the oven, shining your shoes—what's the occasion? I mean, what's all this for?

JOHNNY

Don't you like the flowers?

CELIA

Of course, I like the flowers. I didn't expect to find you home, flowers and the floor mopped.

JOHNNY

You just said that.

CELIA

Said what?

JOHNNY

Flowers and the floor mopped, you said that twice.

CELIA

All right, supposing I did say that twice, what difference does it make!

JOHNNY

No difference, I wasn't criticizing you, I was just—

CELIA

Can we forget it, Johnny, please?

JOHNNY

Forget what?

CELIA

That I said something twice!

JOHNNY

What is it? I was out last night again, is that it?

CELIA

No.

JOHNNY

How many more guesses do I get?

CELIA

It's over.

JOHNNY

What's over? What are you talking about?

CELIA

We've tried.

JOHNNY

I'm behind the times. I thought it was just going to begin. What you said yesterday, that I never came home . . . all the things you said, I've been thinking about them.

CELIA

I'll leave tonight.

JOHNNY

Is it because I lost my job?

CELIA

It's not the job, Johnny.

JOHNNY

What is it?

CELIA

I don't love you.

JOHNNY

And we snap our fingers and that's that?

CELIA

That's the way it is.

JOHNNY

I don't like this talk. Everything's so cold. What is this, a formal dance or something?

CELIA

Johnny, I refuse to get emotional. . . . I just refuse to. My mind is made up. It's not easy, but it's something that has to be done. Now I refuse to get emotional. I'm not going to blame you for anything and I don't want to be blamed for anything. We have to concede that the marriage has failed, not you, not I . . . but we have. I refuse to get emotional. Nothing will be settled by emotion.

JOHNNY

A day isn't just a day, that's what you said. It's not my day or your day. It's not just you and I now.

CELIA

If I understand you correctly, you are talking about the baby?

JOHNNY

Yeh, you understand me correctly.

CELIA

It's amazing, honestly.

JOHNNY

What's amazing? What?

CELIA

For four months I've been waiting for you to say something, one word, one syllable about the baby.

JOHNNY

Today isn't yesterday . . . things can change, you know?

CELIA

Johnny. I don't want to talk any more because I don't want to get emotional.

JOHNNY

I'm home! Do you understand that? I'm home now! I haven't been but I am now. Here! I bought this today.
(*Gives package to her.*)

CELIA

What is it?

JOHNNY

You said it was going to be a girl, didn't you? Five dresses, one for every day of the week . . . that's another thing I did today.

CELIA

Where did you get the money?

JOHNNY

We don't need electric orange-juice squeezers. I can squeeze oranges with my hands.

CELIA

Well, thank you, Johnny. Thank you very much.

JOHNNY

Look, it's my turn to cry, to beg . . . you reached out your hand and I turned my back, you've looked at me and I've closed my eyes. You're not listening to me. Please listen to me. . . . Please.

CELIA

I'm listening.

JOHNNY

All right, you don't love me any more. There was something in me worthwhile loving. You must have loved me for some reason! What was the reason? Celia? Celia? I haven't even used your name. I say baby . . . and I say honey . . . but now I'm saying Celia. Celia. I love you.

CELIA

Oh, Johnny, please. Please stop . . . please.

JOHNNY

I know I've been deaf, dumb and blind but please don't do to me what I did to you. Something happened to me. It's something that's hard to understand. Honey, I don't know whether I'm laughing or crying, but, Celia, you don't have to love me . . . not for a long time. You just don't even have to bother . . .

CELIA

Oh . . . oh . . . oh . . . Do you want to feel something? Johnny, give me your hand . . . Lightly, do you feel it . . . (*She has taken* JOHNNY'S *hand and put it gently over her stomach*) You see?

123

JOHNNY

Oh—Wow! Holy cats . . . I felt it move. I swear I felt it move. Let me feel that again. I don't feel anything. What happened?

CELIA

Nothing happened. It doesn't move all day long. Just every once in a while.

JOHNNY

Well, let me know the next time you think it's going to move.

CELIA

I will.

JOHNNY

That's a real miracle, you know. Heh . . .

CELIA

Hold me, Johnny. Please . . . hold me.

JOHNNY

Oh, you're going to see some changes . . . I've been making plans all day. I've been like a kid waiting for you to come home. I kept looking at the clock.

CELIA

I don't have a handkerchief.

124

JOHNNY

You're not going to leave me? Are you? Tell me?

CELIA

No, Johnny, I'm gonna get an apron.
(POLO *comes in*.)

POLO

The old man's down in Garrity's. He wants to buy you a drink.

JOHNNY

Is he sore?

POLO

He says he wants bygones to be bygones.

JOHNNY

You got a little windburn. Who won the game?

POLO

Who played?

JOHNNY

What's eating you?

POLO

The old man. He thinks I still have that money . . . on the way home he started talking it up again. Gone where? You didn't buy a new car, what do you pay—five hundred dollars a week board? This time he's using the happy-time-U.S.A. approach.

JOHNNY

I'll go down and talk to him.

CELIA

I want you to forget this morning, Polo.

POLO

All right.

JOHNNY

What are you two talking about?

CELIA

Nothing that concerns you, Johnny.

POLO

It's forgotten. Did you tell her, Johnny? Did you tell her?

CELIA

Now what are you two talking about?

JOHNNY

Nothing that concerns you, honey.

126

POLO

The old man will wait a minute.

JOHNNY

Not now, Polo. I'll take care of it. I give you my word, but not now.

POLO

Johnny, I'm going away. I don't know where. I'd like to leave tonight . . . but I can't.

JOHNNY

Let the old man get on his plane and go back to Palm Beach. He doesn't have to know anything.

CELIA

Know what?

POLO

I'm not leaving her with you, Johnny.

JOHNNY

Will you leave us alone for a minute.

CELIA

Johnny! What's the matter!

POLO

I'll stay, Johnny. I've been part of it.

JOHNNY

Look, Celia—now it's nothing to get excited about. (*From off, we hear the* FATHER'S *whistle*) Will you just sit down for a minute. Polo had the money that the old man wanted, but I took it all.

CELIA

What do you mean?

JOHNNY

Look, honey, I'm . . . the thing is, I . . . I'll go down with the old man. He's whistling.

POLO

Tell her, will you please tell her.

CELIA

What is it?

JOHNNY

Get out of my way, Polo . . . you hear me. Get out of my way!

POLO

I'm not in your way. Go ahead, run.

JOHNNY

Honey, my father's whistling. Will you get away from that door. Let me out.

CELIA

Johnny, you can tell me . . . you can tell me anything. What have you done?

FATHER
(*Off*)

Heh, Johnny . . .

POLO

Nobody's going to hate you, Johnny.

FATHER
(*Off*)

Heh, Johnny boy . . .

JOHNNY

Honey, I'm hooked . . . I'm a junkey . . . I take dope. I'm hooked.

CELIA

You're what?

JOHNNY

I'm hooked!

CELIA

That's silly.

JOHNNY

No, it's not silly. I need it, two times . . . every day . . . and it costs money.

CELIA

It's all right. Whatever it is, it's all right. It's all right.

JOHNNY

Don't say anything to the old man.

CELIA

We'll call a doctor.

JOHNNY

Not until the old man goes. He doesn't have to know.

CELIA

Johnny, it doesn't matter. There's nothing to be ashamed of, it's all right, everything's going to be all right.
(FATHER *comes in.*)

FATHER

Where the hell were you? I been downstairs whistling my brains out.

JOHNNY

I didn't hear you, Pop.

FATHER

Didn't hear you, Pop . . . do you know these bums of mine
. . . these bums . . . ?

CELIA

They're not bums.

FATHER

These bums. I spent more time on the back porch whistling.
I'd get all the cats and the dogs in the neighborhood . . . but
no Johnny, not Polo . . . isn't that right, Johnny?

POLO

That's right, Pop.

FATHER

Got a towel for me, honey? (*Moving off into the john; out of
sight*) Did Johnny ever tell you about the time he was a kid I
came home and found him digging up the backyard? I asked
him what the hell are you doing? Workin', daddy . . . me
workin' . . . I told him the only way you get money in your
pockets is to work. He'd dig a hole, and then look in the pockets,
dig another hole and in the pockets, and no money . . . Johnny
was convinced . . . Work and you make money. One day I
came home and it was raining . . . and there's the little bum
there digging away . . . he had his hat laying alongside a big
empty hole . . . and finally I convinced him not to believe what
I told him in the first place, then . . . he bends down and picks
up his hat—and the water goes running all over him . . . he
worked and worked and all he got was a hatful of rain.

CELIA

I was on time for work today.

POLO

You were?

CELIA

Yes, I was.

POLO

Good!

FATHER

There's no napkins on the table. (*Coming out of the john*)
What's everybody so quiet about . . . ?

CELIA

Pass me the pepper and salt . . . please, Polo.

FATHER

Let me have that salt after you.

JOHNNY

How about you, Polo, you want some salt too?

POLO

It needs it.

JOHNNY

I thought I put salt in.

CELIA

We're putting it in now. It doesn't matter.

FATHER

The soup's flat as Kelsey's.

CELIA

Johnny cooked that soup.

FATHER

Let's not start the Trojan war over a bowl of soup.

JOHNNY

How'd you like the ball game, Pop?

FATHER

When that Snider steps up to the plate . . . he looks like he owns the ball park. How about you, Johnny—do you get out and see a ball game?

JOHNNY

No, Pop, I don't . . .

FATHER

You ought to—get out in the air. Fresh air—it's good for you. What the . . . ? What is this, the last supper? What did I do now? Well, go ahead, you guys . . . Did I say something wrong?

JOHNNY

No—we're all a little tired, that's all . . .

FATHER

Talking in short phrases again? Johnny? All right, yes, Pop, no, Pop—

POLO

It's your imagination . . .

CELIA

Can we just pretend that we are—

FATHER

Will you let me say what I want to say! Now look—last night you gave me a working over, right, Polo? And today you really laced into me. Did you see me walking around with my tail between my legs? You didn't come through with the money you promised me. We're eating here now—we're all together, now for crissakes let's have a song or something. Let's get a few laughs . . .

JOHNNY

I'm a junkey, Pop . . .

CELIA

Johnny's sick . . .

FATHER

You don't know what you're talking about . . .

POLO

He knows what he's talking about . . .

FATHER

You mean you take . . . dope? That's a junkey, isn't it?

JOHNNY

That's it.

FATHER

You've known about this, Polo?

POLO

All the time . . .

FATHER

Well, where do you get it . . . I mean, how?

135

POLO

Let's forget it.

FATHER

I'm asking your brother a question. I'm not asking you for orders . . .
(CELIA *moves off into the living room.*)

POLO

I'm giving you one—shut up!

FATHER

Don't say "shut up" to me.

POLO

Keep your hat on.

FATHER

What do you mean, "keep my hat on?"

JOHNNY

Geez, I'm not so hungry. (*Calls to* CELIA) Honey, why don't you sit down and try to eat . . .

CELIA

I was looking for lipstick on your shirts.

FATHER

All the time you knew it . . . ? How long is all the time?

JOHNNY

I've been hooked . . . this time, seven months . . .

FATHER

This time? There was another time . . . ?

JOHNNY

Yeh . . . for a few months after I came out of the hospital, but I told Polo, and he helped me. I kicked it . . .

FATHER

You kicked it . . .

JOHNNY

Yeh, I kicked it . . . I got off the habit.

CELIA

Johnny, please! Don't start getting touchy!

JOHNNY

Well, go to a public library and read up on it! What do you expect me to do, sit here and—

FATHER

Look, I'm going to find out now whose fault this is and who's to blame. And you knew about it, so you talk.

POLO

I don't know whose fault it is. . . .

CELIA

What difference does it make who's to blame. Maybe it's my fault?

FATHER

You're his wife! What do you know about this? You been sleeping in the same bed with him and you don't even know you been sleeping with a dope addict!

POLO

Pop, will you shut up.

CELIA

I haven't been sleeping with a dope addict. We've just been sharing the bed for—

FATHER

For crissakes, it's disgusting. You sit down to dinner and your kid turns out to be a—

JOHNNY

Will you lay off.

CELIA

Why don't you tell me?

JOHNNY

I told you.

FATHER

I can't understand how a boy like you—

JOHNNY

Will you be quiet! And don't turn your back on me like I'm dead . . . I know what I am.

FATHER

What are you?

JOHNNY

I'm a *junkey!*

FATHER

I ought to beat the hell out of you!

POLO

Pop, the kid is trying . . .

FATHER

How could you sit at that table . . . ?

POLO

(*Between* JOHNNY *and the enraged* FATHER)
Lay off him . . . come on now . . .

FATHER

Mind your own business!

CELIA

Please, please . . .

JOHNNY

I'm asking you to be quiet, Pop, I'm not begging . . . Be quiet!

FATHER

Polo, get out of my way . . .

JOHNNY

You raise that hand to me and I'll—

FATHER

Polo, get out of my way—

POLO

He told you, Pop . . .

JOHNNY

I'm trying to tell you something, Pop . . .

POLO

He told you—and telling you hasn't changed anything. He's still a junkey . . . For crissakes he's sick . . . don't you understand that he's sick . . . ?

JOHNNY

I'm not . . . I'm not . . . Oh, what the hell's the use.
   (*He rushes out.*)

FATHER

Johnny, come back here . . . ! Come back! Come back!

CELIA

Johnny . . . Johnny—oh, Johnny, I'm afraid.

POLO

He'll come back . . .

FATHER

He ran away.

POLO

I'll go out and find him.

CELIA

No, Polo. Don't leave me. Stay right here. Just let me sit for a minute. Something is wrong . . .

POLO

The baby?

CELIA

Polo? I think you'd better call a cab . . . Something is going wrong inside of me. I'm afraid to move. . . .

POLO

Get her coat, Pop.
(POLO *runs downstairs.*)

CELIA

He'll come back. He's got to come back . . .

FATHER

Put your arms around me. (*He picks her up*) Just hold tight
. . .

POLO

Taxi! Yo . . . Yo . . . taxi . . . heh, taxi!
(*The* FATHER *moves with* CELIA *toward the door*.)

FATHER

Shhhhh . . . shhhhh. . . .

Curtain

ACT THREE

ACT THREE

When the curtain rises, there are no lights in the apartment area. We see the glow of the skylight. In the distance we hear MOTHER *and* APPLES *laughing hysterically as they climb up the stairs. Their laughter suggests that they are having difficulty in climbing the stairs, probably falling against the wall in hysterics. Finally they appear, their laughter subsiding somewhat.* CHUCH *lags behind.* MOTHER *and* APPLES *walk directly to the door but* CHUCH *starts up the ladder.* MOTHER *turns and calls to him as he knocks on the door.*

MOTHER

Where you going, dummy? Come here . . .

CHUCH

I tole ya I'm not hittin' Johnny.

MOTHER
(*Calling*)
Heh, Johnny . . . it's your old Mother.

CHUCH

You said I don't have to hit him . . .

147

MOTHER

(*Knocking*)

Will you shut up . . . !

APPLES

He ain't home.

CHUCH

Come on, let's go.

MOTHER

Cross the roof . . . come in the fire escape, Chuchie . . . and open the door.

CHUCH

All right. . . .
(*He scurries up the fire escape.*)

APPLES

You gonna sweat him out? Huh, Mother . . . ?

MOTHER

We gonna sweat him out.

APPLES

You know what I like about you, Mother?

MOTHER

What do you like about me?

APPLES

I'm gonna tell you what I like about you.

MOTHER

What?

APPLES

No matter what the band plays . . . you hear your own music.

MOTHER

That stuff was a hundred per cent pure. Man, I feel like King Kong ridin' a cloud . . .
    (MOTHER *opens the door and they both enter.*)

CHUCH

    (*Coming from the other side*)
That door was open there all the time!

MOTHER

Chuch, I goofed. What are you doing?

CHUCH

I'm sitting down.

MOTHER

I know you're sitting down. Go down to the car and keep an eye on that whacky broad . . .

CHUCH

Make Apples go down. I don't want to go near that whacky broad. She's always trying to grab me . . .

MOTHER

Well, let her grab you, but keep an eye on her . . .

CHUCH

I always get the short end . . .
(CHUCH *goes out. The phone rings,* APPLES *picks it up.*)

APPLES

Hold on a minute, willya . . . It's Ginnino . . . No, nothing happened. No, I'm not laughin' at you, Mother's startin' to float. Yeh . . . huh, yeh. Man, we almost got arrested four times today, and the day's not over yet. Mother's floatin' away, and he ain't coming back. . . .

MOTHER

Lay down the red carpet for our man.

APPLES

Heh, little Jim . . . Mother and me and that whacky broad, the one with all the money. We're going up to Connecticut . . .

Her family went to Europe. She's out in the car now . . . with
no clothes on. They raided the hotel she's at . . . and she had to
run . . . she got no clothes on. Man, are you crazy? She got a
coat on . . .

PUTSKI

(*Enters hurriedly,* CHUCH *following her*)
Don't touch me . . . He tried to touch me . . . I was sitting
lighting a cigarette and he grabbed the inside of my leg and I
won't stand for it. After all, it's my car.

CHUCH

I didn't try to touch her. She grabbed me. . . .

PUTSKI

I don't want to go down to the car . . . I'll just sit here like
the Queen Mother and not say a word.

APPLES

Where's your place in Connecticut . . . ?

PUTSKI

Just outside of Greenwich . . . and it's not my place, it's
Lester's place, Lester's the man Mummy married since Daddy
disappeared. . . .

APPLES

There's five bathrooms in the house. One for everybody . . .
No, man, we're looking to collect some money. Right, Mother.

MOTHER

Right. Money or the lumps.

APPLES

Little Jim wants to know if we pick him up on the way.

MOTHER

He's with us.

APPLES

As soon as we can, man . . . sit tight and hold right . . . right? And there you go, Jim!

MOTHER

What time is it, Apples . . . ?

APPLES

My clock says eleven o'clock . . .

MOTHER

That's a nice clock you got there . . .

APPLES

I mean watcht. I allus say clock . . .

MOTHER

Yeh, an you *allus* say *axt*. It's *ask* with a K, not axt, you silly bastard . . .

APPLES

Wait a minute, teacher. I'll ring the bell and get the rest of the kids in. . . .

(*Everything becomes unusually silent for a good minute.* PUTSKI *is back in a chair, staring dreamily at the ceiling.* APPLES *hums, "like a saxophone";* MOTHER *stands doing absolutely nothing. Only* CHUCH *looks about wondering why a silence has descended . . . all being addicted and under the influence of drugs, their sense of time becomes peculiar, not noticeable to themselves, but to an onlooker they appear to be either in slow motion or hopped. There is a sense of a vacuum . . . and then, coming from nowhere a sense of chaos and speed.* MOTHER *sits, takes out a book and reads as though he were in the public library.*)

CHUCH

What are we doin'?

APPLES

We're waitin' . . .

CHUCH

What are we waitin' for?

APPLES

The money—we're waitin' for the money.

153

CHUCH

Oh. . . .

PUTSKI

I can't stand people who feel a compulsion to talk endlessly . . .

APPLES

What are you reading? You're allus readin' . . . He allus reading, Chuch. You remember what happened to Crazy Stanley.

CHUCH

Yeh . . . Crazy Stanley was allus readin'. I saw him flip. He never read comic books. Always readin' about the planets, rocket ships.

APPLES

You hear that, Mother?

MOTHER

Yeh . . .

APPLES

Keep on readin'. Just keep on readin' . . .

MOTHER

You ever thought about committing suicide, Apples?

APPLES

No, man, I'm young yet. I'm only nineteen . . .

CHUCH

Will you guys shut up!

APPLES

You know something, Chuch? You ugly.

MOTHER

Apples is right, Chuch. You're ugly . . .

APPLES

You can't help it if you're ugly, Chuch. Mother's ugly too, but it doesn't bother him. . . .

MOTHER

You know something, Apples, you're getting disrespectful just because we're friends, and you know something else, you'd better have eyes in the back of your head when you start getting disrespectful. . . .

APPLES

Take it easy, Brother Mother.

MOTHER

Don't butter me, Apples. Get your hands out of your pockets. And don't turn your back because I'll punch you right in the back.

CHUCH

Go ahead, kill each other. Go ahead. There's seven million people in this city, and we have to fight each other. Go ahead, I don't know whose side I'm going to be on, start punching I'll pick a side.

MOTHER

Chuch, do yourself a favor.

CHUCH

Mother, do me a favor? Just do me a favor. Don't start puttin' ideas in my head.

APPLES

Take it easy, Chuch, we ain't gonna steal nothin'. We're going to Connecticut . . .

CHUCH

He sees an ole lady pushin' a baby carriage around at night collecting newspapers . . . an' a bell goes off. Some people got water on the knee, and he's got hermits on the brain. . . .

MOTHER

What are you talking about, Chuch?

CHUCH

You told me I can't keep chasin' the tiger's tail. I got to lock horns if I want to get my fix! You told me where she kept the money . . . out of the frying pan and into the gold-plated casserole. I could sleep tight if I had a bundle of thousands under my pillow . . . huh?

MOTHER

We're gonna go to Connecticut. They got an A.S.P.C.A. in Connecticut.

CHUCH

Go by the A.S.P.C.A.? The cops come two hours after he died . . . and then the A.S.P.C.A. truck come too. The cop says the dog is dead. He died in my arms and he tells me the dog is dead. . . . I says to the guy from the A.S.P.C.A.—What'll I do with him? Throw him in the garbage, he says, we don't take the dead ones . . . that's for the sanitation department.

MOTHER

Huh, Chuchie Duchie . . . you can buy a cocker spaniel for ten bucks . . . !

CHUCH

Three dollars and sixteen cents . . . three dollars and sixteen cents! That's all. . . . God punished me.
(JOHNNY *bursts in the door. A* MAN *slides down the ladder and plants himself in the hallway.*)

MAN

Back up, Johnny . . . back up like a mule.

157

CHUCH

I killed the old lady, Johnny. I didn't mean to kill her. He wouldn't give me no more credit. Three dollars and sixteen cents!

MOTHER

You got the eight hundred . . . ?

JOHNNY

Where's my wife . . . ?

MOTHER

Button up your buttons, honey, we're getting out of here. . . .

CHUCH

Johnny, you look bad. . . .

JOHNNY

I'll be all right. . . .

CHUCH

Yeh, sure, but three dollars and sixteen cents. I didn't mean to do it.
(*Goes off, mumbling.*)

MOTHER

Button 'em up.

PUTSKI

I had the most wonderful dream. . . .

MOTHER

Get her down to the car. I'll take care of Johnny. . . .

PUTSKI

I'm not moving until it's perfectly understood that everyone will have their own room . . . and there'll be no going from one room to another . . . I hope no one here had any ideas about me . . . because they're completely mistaken. . . .

APPLES

Come on, nobody's got any ideas about you. . . .

MOTHER

Get her down to the car. . . .

PUTSKI

(*Going out*)

It has to be perfectly understood that the run of the premises are yours—you can eat until your hearts are content . . . but there'll be no fooling around, no voyages from one room to another. Hey, who's that guy?

MOTHER

Come here, Junkey—I'm not going to hurt you. I'm not greedy. Come here, I want to give you something . . . honest.

You're sick, Junkey . . . can you see me way over here? I'm smiling.

JOHNNY

You'll get your eight hundred . . . every lousy cent of it.

MOTHER

Your word is your bond, my man—you know how to use that thing you've got in your hand—Hey, can you see me over here? Look, pure white—a free ride on the midnight carousel, tax free, on the house.

JOHNNY

I'm through!

MOTHER

No more trying to get the things you wanted all your life . . . and you fly, Johnny, like a bird.

JOHNNY

I'm through, Mother, I'm quitting.
(POLO *enters.*)

POLO

Heh, Mother . . . There's eight hundred . . . Count it downstairs, will you?

MOTHER

He'll crawl . . .
> (*He goes out.*)

JOHNNY

Where's Celia . . . ?

POLO

She'll be here . . .

JOHNNY

Did you put the old man on his plane . . . ?

POLO

Where you going?

JOHNNY

I'm a half-hour from hell, Polo. I'm going up to the St. Nicholas and get myself a room. I'm going to kick it. . . .

POLO

I was in that room with you once before, Johnny . . .

JOHNNY

I lock myself up for three days . . . and I won't touch a thing. When I come out, I'll be straight again . . .

POLO

You won't last a day in that room . . .

JOHNNY

Come with me. You come with me . . . you watch me. You can keep me locked up for three days . . . That's all it takes, Polo. Three lousy days . . .

POLO

Johnny, I can't watch you go through that again . . .

JOHNNY

I did it once before—and I'll do it again.

POLO

Listen, Johnny—I held you down on that bed for three days! Maybe you can go through that hell again, but I can't watch you again . . . Johnny, sit down, willya . . . ?

JOHNNY

Polo, my time's running out . . .

POLO

Listen to me . . . Celia almost lost the baby. She's all right . . . take it easy. We left her at the doctor's . . . He wanted her to lay down for an hour. She knows you don't have to run any more . . .

JOHNNY

She's all right . . . ? Don't lie to me, Polo . . .

POLO

I just called the doctor's—she's on her way home.

JOHNNY

And the old man . . . ?

POLO

I told him I paid for it, Johnny—in the doctor's office. And I left him sitting there . . . saying, no, no, no, no, Polo, you couldn't do that to your brother . . .

JOHNNY

They'll be coming here . . .

POLO

You couldn't walk one block.

JOHNNY

Polo, I got to get out of here. I can't let them see me like this . . . Polo, I'm quitting, don't you believe me?

POLO

For the first time, I do. I know you can do it . . .

JOHNNY

Then for the last time, Polo, help me. Get a cab. Get me out of here. Polo, I don't want them to see me!

POLO

All right, Johnny, I'll go with you. I'll do what I have to do.

JOHNNY

It's starting, Polo . . . it's starting. Oh God . . .

FATHER
(*Knocks on door*)

Polo? Polo? Open the door . . .

POLO

Go in the back room and be quiet . . .
(JOHNNY *goes into the bedroom.*)

FATHER

Polo . . . !

POLO
(*Going to door*)

I'm sorry, Pop, I . . .

FATHER

Did you find him? Did you find your brother Johnny?

POLO

No, Pop—did you go to all the places I told you to go?

FATHER

Nobody's seen him . . .

POLO

Celia'll be right home—I called her.

FATHER

It's a good thing that was a false alarm, Polo.

POLO

She's all right. She's on her way home.

FATHER

Where are you going?

POLO

Pop, your plane leaves in an hour.

FATHER

Planes fly every day. Where you going? You want to get out of here now, huh? That's all you want. Three thousand dollars' worth of poison in your brother's arm and you paid for it!

POLO

Twenty-five hundred.

FATHER

That was the right thing to do? Help your brother kill himself. You have an alibi . . . What have you got to say for yourself?

POLO

Nothing.

FATHER

What have you got to say to me?

POLO

Get on your plane and go back to Palm Beach where everything is nice and quiet. Come on, Pop—I want you to get out of here.

FATHER

Get away from that bag, and don't call me Pop. Let's just be two men talking. Talk to me like I'm your brother. You'll get out of here, maybe not on your own two feet, but you'll get out of here.

POLO

Take it easy, Pop.

FATHER

I'm getting red in the face, huh? Maybe I'd better sit down. I'm not as young as I used to be. I'm soft, not hard enough for you.

POLO

Now, look, Pop, you don't know what you're doing.

FATHER

Where's your brother? You're not your brother's keeper. Are you going to shut up on me again? You're forgetting I'm your father!

POLO

Well, for crissakes look at you. You don't even know what's happened and you're trying to put the blame somewhere.

FATHER

My son, if you knew how ashamed I was to admit that you're my son. Am I a child? Are you my father? You know what I'm going to do . . . ? You remember once how Pete the big bay horse kicked me and put me in the hospital . . . and when I came out I turned that bastard loose in the barn and locked the doors . . . that ungrateful sonafabitch that I slept in the straw with when he was sick. I fought that horse with my bare hands . . . and you and Johnny were up in the hayloft, yelling, "Look out, Pop . . . that horse is going to kill you!" I'm going to beat you, Polo! And you can punch back, like he kicked back. You fight back. Take your coat off.

POLO

No, I'm not going to take my coat off. You couldn't hurt me any more if you killed me. Listen. You were two thousand miles away but I was here. You told me a hundred times in every letter you ever wrote that I should fall on my hands and knees and light twenty candles a day because my brother had taken me in.

FATHER

You couldn't write to me and tell me?

POLO

Write to you and tell you what? That your favorite son was a goddamned junkey. You going to swing. Swing! Take your failures out on me . . . and when you finish I'm going to tell you where your son is . . . I took care of him . . . I'm my brother's keeper more than you know. (*The* FATHER *swings and hits* POLO *soundly across the face with an open hand*) You poor old man. What are you hitting me for? What have I done? You walk around with your head in the clouds. Why don't you stand still for a minute and try to find something out?

FATHER

Dope? Junkey? And you paid for it?
(*The kitchen door opens and* CELIA *enters.*)

CELIA

Johnny—Johnny—Where's Johnny?

POLO

He's not here. We looked all over, we couldn't find him. Isn't that right, Pop?

CELIA

I don't know who his friends are, Polo. You'd know that. There were two men here last night. What were their names?

FATHER

I don't know. One of them had on glasses.

POLO

Are you all right?

CELIA

I won't be all right until I see Johnny.

FATHER

He knows where he is . . .

POLO

What did the doctor say?

CELIA

My baby is all right.

169

POLO

This isn't the place to be. All you have to do is get out of here for a few—

CELIA

I live here and I'm staying here. I'm all right and I won't scream or cry, but are you all right, Polo? Are you?

POLO

You're going to miss your plane, Pop.

FATHER

I told you before, planes fly every day.

CELIA

Where is my husband?

POLO

He's waiting for me. He asked me to keep you and the old man away from him. Don't push me. He'd die of shame if you saw him now, and you'd get sick. I'll be running out in the street looking for a taxi again. I tell you, I know what I'm doing.

CELIA

You don't know what you're doing and don't know what you've done, Polo. I just keep thinking that you hate him—that you hate your brother!

POLO

You know I love him . . .

CELIA

You just don't love. When you love you have to be responsible to what you love.

POLO

He'll help himself—he wants to quit.

CELIA

He'll never do it by himself and you *know* that.

POLO

I don't know that.

CELIA

Polo, don't turn your back, you can look at me. I know you meant well, and that you mean well now, but I talked to my doctor, Polo, there is little any of us can do . . . There is little that all the doctors in the world can do right now but try to help him, and you *know* that. There's a slight chance . . . only a slight one—and don't tell me that you've been feeding him money all this time and that you don't know. You're afraid to admit that. . . .

POLO

Don't you see, as long as he gets it, he's all right. You'd never know he was any different.

CELIA

Polo! You're not two little kids huddled in a dark room any more. I should be angry at you, but I'm not.

POLO

I'm not afraid of anything . . . and I didn't do any wrong. When you have your baby—and if you can imagine for one minute your child writhing in *pain*—and all you have to do is reach out and hand—

CELIA

I'd reach out and stop its crying . . . I'd give it anything it needed but I wouldn't stop there, I'd try to find out what caused the pain—I love your brother Johnny, I have faith in that love. He is a perfect human being, and I'm proud of him, not ashamed of him, and I don't pity him, and I'm not afraid of him . . . and the more I see you now, the more I realize that your love is irresponsible. Now you tell me where he is, Polo, or I'll call the police and have them find him . . .

FATHER

You'd call the police, you're so proud of him . . .

CELIA

I'm not a member of your vacuum age, Mr. Pope. And I'm sorry I cannot regard you as his father at this moment; unfortunately you are just another man . . .

172

A HATFUL OF RAIN

FATHER

No. No police. We'll get a doctor . . .

CELIA

They'd only have to call the police. Isn't that right, Polo?

FATHER

But we can take care of him together. I don't have to go back
to Palm Beach, I can get a good job up here. We can all take
care of him together. You don't have to call the police . . .

CELIA

There's a place in Kentucky that takes care of people like
Johnny.

FATHER

What people like Johnny? Who do you think you're talking
about? There's nothing wrong with him! What the hell—
people drink, don't they? So he takes a little something once in
a while, what are you running to the police for . . . ?

JOHNNY

(*Off*)

Polo! (*Comes in*) Get them out of here, get them out of here.
I don't want them to see me like this.

173

FATHER

Johnny . . .

JOHNNY

Pop. Watch over me—watch over me. Don't let them come near me again. Don't let me go, willya, Pop.

FATHER

For crissakes, Polo, he's dying. He's freezing—what do we do?

POLO

Hold on, for the love of God, hold on. We're all here . . .

FATHER

Easy, Johnny, easy . . . Polo, what do I do?

POLO

Rock him—rock him like a baby in your arms. Hold him, hold him tight and never let him go. Rock him, you rock him, Pop, I rocked him long enough, you watch over him!

JOHNNY

Celia, Celia, Celia. I didn't want you to see this. I didn't want anybody to see this.

174

CELIA

Well, we've seen it, Johnny, and we can't just make believe
we didn't, can we?

JOHNNY

Pop, I'm sorry about all that . . . all that—you know. Next
time I open my mouth . . . you just haul off and give me a belt.

FATHER

Okay, kid.

JOHNNY

Pop, will you please go; I want to be alone with my wife.

FATHER

Yeh—You want to walk me over to the hotel, Polo?

POLO

Yeh, come on . . .
      (POLO *starts to leave.*)

FATHER

Good night, honey . . .
      (*Goes out.*)

CELIA

Good night, Pop. Come over for breakfast, please.

POLO

(*From the doorway*)
You'll be all right, Johnny.
(*He leaves with* FATHER.)

JOHNNY

Hey—Pop—hey—if you drop your hat crossing the—Celia, I'm sorry, you don't know how sorry I am . . .

CELIA

I don't care how sorry you are, Johnny. I want to call the police and I want you to go into a hospital. I'm going to call them, no matter what you say, darling. We can't live like this, can we? You can live or die . . .

JOHNNY

I'm all right. It's so unbelievable. To know everything that's right. Thou shalt not kill or walk on the grass; I've been taught everything good . . . Make the phone call . . .

CELIA

Give me the police . . . I'd like to report a drug addict. My husband. Yes, he's here now. Would you send over whoever you send in a case like this—and try to hurry, please. Thank you. Mrs. Celia Pope, 967 Rivington Street . . . fourth flight up. And would you hurry, please . . . Thank you.

Curtain